LEARN to

LAUNCH

LEARN to

LAUNCH

A Guide to Starting New Projects

ROBERT B. SOWBY

Learn to Launch: A Guide to Starting New Projects

Second Printing 2021

ISBN 978-1-387-08022-9

Do not go where the path may lead, go instead where there is no path and leave a trail.

Attributed to RALPH WALDO EMERSON

Contents

Introduction

Off the Ground

In the long run, men hit only what they aim at.
Therefore, though they should fail immediately,
they had better aim at something high.

HENRY DAVID THOREAU[1]

A s a boy I watched the sky: planes and birds by day, and stars and satellites by night. I often dreamed of becoming a pilot or an astronaut, soaring above the Rocky Mountains or boldly exploring the universe.

My maternal grandfather, Robert Paul "Bob" Williams, was a World War II veteran and retired corporate pilot. He had enlisted in the Navy and during the war had been stationed in Recife, Brazil, where he served as chief of an amphibious "flying boat" patrolling for German submarines off the coast. He took flying lessons from a native Brazilian pilot who spoke little English; they communicated mostly with gestures and hand signals. Grandpa was hooked. He earned his first pilot's license about the same time he married my grandmother in 1944. He later became a flight instructor, charter pilot, and corporate pilot, flying more than 15,000 hours (two full years!) in 50 different types of aircraft by the time he retired.[2]

Until about age six, I spent many Saturday afternoons in Grandpa Williams's suburban Salt Lake City garage, full with the scent of dust and oil, where, now in retirement, he was building his own flashy aerobatic biplane. Narrow red and yellow pinstripes lined the white fuselage, like ribbons of ketchup and mustard delicately applied to a giant, pale bratwurst. I used to sit in the cockpit and "practice flying" while Grandpa tuned up the engine or tested the ailerons. His suave silvery hair and tanned skin complemented the sturdy figure of a war veteran, the very image of vigor, even in supposed retirement. He regularly escorted us grandkids and our cousins on hiking and camping adventures. Even when talking to himself while fussing over nuts and bolts in his garage, his rich baritone bore the wisdom of a grandfather and the enthusiasm of an explorer. His sleeves were usually rolled up to expose the strong, skilled hands of a craftsman—the same hands that had chopped firewood and fed babies with equal skill. Regardless of how many appliances he had repaired, camping trips he had led, or corporate flights he had piloted, this biplane was Grandpa's biggest project yet. It was exciting for all of us.

When finally assembled, the plane flew only a few times. One of its first voyages was, unfortunately, its final voyage, when my 68-year-old grandfather likely blacked out from a stroke and fatally crashed in a field outside of town.[3] But at least it got off the ground, and Bob Williams was pursuing his dream.

Grandpa Williams in his biplane.

Later, in elementary school, I built model rockets. I studied the manufacturers' catalogs and gawked at the rocketry selection in our local hobby store. When I was able to purchase a kit on occasion, upon returning home, I would blaze through the house and burst into by bedroom above the garage to begin assembly. I didn't even need the instructions—I already knew how it all fit together. My first model, the Helicat, was a slender yellow rocket about three feet tall, with four black fins and a detachable nose. The nose featured three spring-loaded helicopter blades that would deploy to ease its descent, while a small parachute carried the body. Another rocket, the Payloader, had a clear plastic segment for electronics, glow sticks, cheese, insects, and other willing subjects of my high-acceleration micro-experiments. My smallest projectile, called the Mosquito, looked like a pointy dry-erase marker with three caudal fins. Astronomy posters, science books, and a supply of model glue, solid-fuel engines, and spare decals completed my above-the-garage rocket studio.

Toting my rockets and launch apparatus in a squeaky wagon, I shot off my rockets after hours in the schoolyard. I also brought sundry homemade instruments to capture flight data. Two yardsticks and a length of yarn, all hinged end to end, formed an oversized inclinometer with which I could measure the angle between my observation point and the rocket's apex, enabling me to compute its final altitude. I clocked the burn time and fall time with a lanyard stopwatch from my father's marathon days. A wisp of paper affixed to the end of a pencil was my wind gauge, with the direction inferred from my Boy Scout compass. Monitoring and calculating with all the rigor of a ten-year-old, I tried to predict an exact landing site for each rocket. Even with help from my engineer father, my predictions were never accurate—there were simply too many variables—and many a rocket (including the Mosquito, may it rest in pieces) was lost to trees or powerlines or ditches. But at least they got off the ground, and I was pursuing my dream.

Orville and Wilbur Wright's first airplane flight on December 17, 1903, was a turning point of history and the beginning of greater change than they could have imagined. And what a change it was already from their modest beginnings. Historian David McCullough wrote of the brothers' incredibly slim odds of success:

> They had had no college education, no formal technical training, no experience working with anyone other than themselves, no friends in high places, no financial backers, no government subsidies, and little money of their own. [There was also] the entirely real possibility that at some point ... they could be killed.[4]

By common-sense standards, they had no chance at all. Yet the two tenacious gentlemen from Dayton, Ohio, solved one unforeseen problem after another—lift, control, and propulsion, just to name a few—to finally develop and later master a new technology.

Their first true flight, on North Carolina's Outer Banks, was brief but monumental. "It was only a flight of twelve seconds," Orville said afterward, "and it was an uncertain, wavy, creeping sort of flight at best, but it was a real flight at last."[5] At least it got off the ground, and they were pursuing their dream.

The Wright Brothers' flight, Dec. 17, 1903. It was the first flight of a manned, self-powered, heavier-than-air machine.

A new project is like an airplane or rocket. It may be someone's dream and it needs to go somewhere, but it must first get off the ground. It needs a launch. Too many projects don't even make it as far as my grandfather's biplane or my model rockets or the 1903 Wright Flyer. They can't even leave the ground, let alone soar to their destiny. What holds them back, and how to overcome it, is the subject of *Learn to Launch*.

I began exploring the topic after personally observing several project launches (or project kickoffs) since I started college. Before becoming a full-time water resources engineer after graduating from the Massachusetts Institute of Technology, I had worked several smaller jobs while attending Brigham Young University. I was a teaching assistant in the Marriott School of Management, research assistant in the Civil Engineering department, administrative assistant in the McKay School of Education's dean's office, Utah Valley Symphony publicist, geotechnical laboratory technician, and later a freelance business writer and software developer. I also served in various assignments in my local congregation of The Church of Jesus Christ of Latter-day Saints.

While I don't usually list these smaller experiences on my résumé, they are important for another reason: such diverse jobs allowed me to experience many types of projects and launches. Whether observing or participating, I spent those years weaving through new education initiatives, health products, construction projects, mobile apps, and scores of other assorted projects. Some crashed, some wobbled, and some flew. Some never took off. Since starting my engineering career and taking on other volunteer church assignments, I've been involved in many more launches at closer scales and with more responsibility, but I still observed the same irregular behavior. Why did some projects appear to fly so immediately while others shuddered into low orbit or burned on the launch pad? The project's size didn't seem to matter; large and small projects were equally vulnerable. Even well-funded projects led by experienced managers weren't guaranteed a smooth launch. Academic, professional, and church settings seemed to make little difference. Some projects had exciting and important goals but still flopped. What was wrong?

Over time, among these diverse projects, I began to notice certain patterns that corresponded to successful launches and, subsequently, successful projects. Soon I realized that

Though this be madness, yet there is method in't.[6]

I compared my observations with case studies and published literature. Through small projects at work, home, church, and school, I tested and refined my theories. Some factors I had initially considered broke down or turned out to be superficial manifestations of a deeper, more fundamental principle. In the end I arrived at three critical components I call the "launch engines": *vision, team,* and *plan.* Every project needs all three engines to succeed, and launch is the time to address them.

Chapter 1 defines what a project is (and isn't), which is an important beginning to understanding how to launch one successfully. Chapter 2 explores why launches fail. Chapter 3 introduces the launch engines and Chapters 4, 5, and 6 discuss them each in more detail. Launch procedures—tips for actually starting the project—are presented in Chapter 7, and Chapter 8 describes how to maintain trajectory after the launch. Throughout the book, I present the launch concepts alongside poetry, research, and case literature. Endnotes direct you to sources, commentary, and further reading. "Launch Logs"—anecdotes from my own experience or that of my direct associates—illustrate the main ideas, though names and other details have been changed to protect identities. "Launch Lessons" at the end of each chapter summarize the key points, and "Action Items" invite you to consider what you'll do with the insight you gain while reading.

Much of modern project management relies on sophisticated tools, software, or products, and many project management books are written to promote their use. While I acknowledge the value of such tools and even use them in my own projects, in *Learn to Launch* I set them all aside in favor of fundamental principles. If you're looking for nifty apps or clever shortcuts, you won't find them here. Yes, you will need some tools to help you along, but I leave it to you to find the best solutions for your project. I avoid cliché business proverbs and, as is currently popular in many business blogs, rebuttals of the same cliché business proverbs. Likewise, I won't offer specific recommendations for setting a budget or negotiating a contract or crafting a meeting agenda. Those details are up to you. Instead, I focus on the principles of the three launch engines and their role in successful projects.

Around Christmas of 2003 I devoted some time to writing poetry, and one subject of interest at the time was the 100th anniversary of the Wrights' first flight. I had recently visited Kitty Hawk, North Carolina, where the Wrights made their early flights. The centennial hype, combined with my interest in aviation, led me to compose the following poem, entitled "Wrights' Legacy":

A hundred years or so have passed
Since two men took to flight,
And made themselves a name to last:
Orville and Wilbur Wright.

At Kitty Hawk, on windswept hills,
With coastal breezes nigh,
The brothers, not without some spills,
Became the first to fly.

The innovative seeds were sown;
At last, the dream came true.
Oh, how the winds of time have blown
Since first the brothers flew!

Today, the Wrights would surely stare
To see what they began:
A million shapes high in the air
From New York to Japan.

These pioneers of flight so grand
Have shaped the course we take,
And through the air, 'cross sea and land,
We follow in their wake.

The brothers' magnificent journey epitomizes the three components so critical for successful launches, both figurative and literal: a vision, a team, and a plan. These are the launch engines, the powerhouses that overcome the gravity of the status quo and propel a project into flight.

The Wrights' project changed the world. Will yours?

NOTES

[1] Henry David Thoreau, *Walden*, ed. Jeffrey S. Kramer (New Haven, CT: Yale University Press, 2006), 27.

[2] The foregoing details of his military service and flying career come from Laurie Williams Sowby, "Life Sketch of Bob Williams," August 20, 1992.

[3] Norma Wagner, "Pilot Killed as Homemade Biplane Crashes in Desert Near Herriman," *Salt Lake Tribune*, August 17, 1992, B1; Joe Costanzo, "W. V. Pilot Dies as Plane Crashes in Dunes," *Deseret News*, August 17, 1992; "Death: 'Bob' Williams." *Salt Lake Tribune*, August 18, 1992, D10. Investigators noted the plane's outstanding workmanship and could find no mechanical failure.

[4] David McCullough, *The Wright Brothers* (New York: Simon & Shuster, 2015), 35.

[5] McCullough, *The Wright Brothers*, 105.

[6] William Shakespeare, *Hamlet, Prince of Denmark*, ed. David Bevington and David Scott Kastan (New York: Bantam Dell, 2005), 2.2.205–206.

Chapter 1

What's a Project?

All there is to thinking is seeing something noticeable
which makes you see something you weren't noticing
which makes you see something that isn't even there.

NORMAN MACLEAN[1]

Intuitively we know what a project is. We deal with them all the time: developing a product, completing a consulting job, or researching a new technology.

But projects come in many sizes and forms. Acknowledging their diversity will expand our view of what projects are and enable us to apply the launch engines in the following chapters to much more that we otherwise would. In this chapter we'll formally define the term and explore the rich variety of projects all around us.

Defining *Project*

While we are familiar with the word *project* by experience, a formal definition from the Oxford Dictionaries will guide our discussion:

> **proj·ect** /ˈprɒdʒɛkt/ NOUN An individual or collaborative enterprise that is carefully planned and designed to achieve a particular aim.[2]

First, a project is an "enterprise": an "undertaking, typically one that is difficult or requires effort."[3] Notice how difficulty and effort are built in to this definition; something that's easy is not a project. In starting a project, you're fighting entropy—the natural tendency toward disorder over order—to organize and focus human, financial, and temporal resources on a specific problem. That requires effort.

The project may be individual, as in starting a blog, or collaborative, as in developing new software. Either way, people are an important ingredient in any project. A proper team is one of the launch engines discussed in Chapters 3 and 5.

Next, a project is "carefully planned." Both words are important. First, the phrase implies that a project is not accidental, spontaneous, off-the-cuff, or otherwise unplanned. It requires planning. Second, not just any planning will do, but *careful* planning. A project involves deliberate and attentive planning of money, time, equipment, and people. The criticality of a project plan, another of the launch engines, is discussed in Chapters 3 and 6.

Finally, and most importantly, a project is "designed to meet a particular aim." Otherwise why do it? A project has specific goals, objectives, or purposes—to produce a unique product, for example—toward which one designs a sequence of organized tasks. As will be discussed later, the aim is often expressed as a vision. Goals define the project's direction and explain why it's necessary: Where are we going and why?

A project without a goal is no project at all. The importance of vision as a launch engine is discussed in Chapters 3 and 4.

Size Doesn't Matter

Notice how the definition gives no size restriction. A project may therefore be large or small or anything in between. It may involve one person or one thousand, last one day or one decade, or cost ten dollars or ten billion dollars. This concept should open our eyes to things we wouldn't otherwise consider projects.

Consider the following examples of smaller projects:

- Writing a memo
- Interviewing a job candidate
- Hosting a meeting or event
- Debugging software
- Preparing a conference presentation
- Upgrading a payment system
- Responding to a customer service request

Wait a minute, you say. Those are just *tasks*. That's true, but individually, they still satisfy the definition of a project by requiring effort, people, planning, and goals. They may be components of larger projects, such as:

- Starting a company
- Acquiring another company
- Debuting a product line
- Running a political campaign
- Advertising a theater season
- Developing software
- Designing an office building

Regardless of size, these are all clearly projects, each one a deliberate solo or group effort with specific goals.

Beyond Business

Until now, all the examples I've used have had a deliberate business slant. But the definition doesn't restrict projects to business or professional pursuits.

While we often refer to projects in the business sense, many, if not most, of the projects we regularly encounter or engage in are found outside the workplace. Your projects at home, school, church, or in the community meet the definition just as well as anything else. As with size, this should expand our perception of projects beyond the workplace.

A project can be anything. Consider the following:

- A bake sale
- A church service
- A concert
- A family vacation
- A football game
- A home remodel
- A new skill
- A dinner party
- A vehicle purchase
- A term paper or thesis

Are these not also projects? They certainly meet the definition. In a bake sale, for example, one undertakes, with others, to raise money by selling baked goods. That's a project.

Projects All Around Us

Had you lived a few centuries ago, you might have thought that biological life was limited to what you could see with your own eyes: humans, animals, plants. But we now know that entire ecosystems exist beyond our natural observational capability: the microscopic world of bacteria. Though we don't think about it or see it, we interact with this world daily, for good or for ill. Bacteria float in the air, crawl on our touchscreens, and work inside our stomachs. They were always there, always a form of life; we just didn't see them or understand their role until we had the right perspective. The biological world is much more extensive than we once thought.

In the same sense, you should see by now that projects of all sizes and forms surround us constantly, and that their extent is much greater than one might realize. The definition suggests, and the explication demonstrates, a multiplicity of projects. We don't just encounter projects at work; we live among them, interact with them, and depend on them, whether we realize it or not.

The principles in this book, specifically the three launch engines discussed later, are not unique to business. As you read, keep in mind how you might use the concepts in not only your next professional project but also your next bake sale, family vacation, or vehicle purchase.

Their universal applicability is perhaps the launch engines' greatest strength: they work for any project, large or small, in business or beyond, to power a successful launch.

Launch Lessons

- A project requires effort, people, careful planning, and specific goals.
- Projects take on many sizes, from brief individual tasks to large organizational undertakings.
- Projects take on many forms beyond the workplace, including those at home, school, church, or in the community.

- Understanding project variety helps us apply the principles discussed in later chapters.

Action Items

Based on what I learned from this chapter, I will:

_____

_____

_____

_____

_____

_____

NOTES

[1] Norman Maclean, *A River Runs Through It, and Other Stories* (Chicago: University of Chicago Press, 1976), 92.

[2] *Oxford Dictionaries*, s.v. "project," accessed July 18, 2016, http://www.oxforddictionaries.com/.

[3] *Oxford Dictionaries*, s.v. "enterprise," accessed July 18, 2016, http://www.oxforddictionaries.com/.

Chapter 2

Why Do Launches Fail?

Everything would be so nice
If only one could do things twice.

JOHANN WOLFGANG VON GOETHE[1]

A t age 11, I witnessed a real rocket launch at Cape Canaveral: NASA's STS-91 (Space Transportation System), the space shuttle *Discovery*'s final docking with the Russian space station *Mir*.[2] NASA and other groups had been preparing for STS-91 well before the launch, of course. It was a project. Reflecting on the definition of *project* given in Chapter 1, the mission was defined (a "particular aim"), a crew selected ("collaborative"), and a flight plan approved ("carefully planned"), not to mention the copious effort invested in the entire space shuttle program to date (an "enterprise").

On launch day, at a viewpoint several miles away, my father and I leaned over a roadside fence and awaited the countdown. My attention was fixed on the distant launch pad, where seven brave astronauts sat atop 2.6 million pounds of solid and liquid rocket fuel. The spacecraft was loaded with thousands of pounds of water, scientific equipment, and supplies for its nine-day, 3.8-million-mile mission, orbiting over 200 miles above the Earth.

Despite all I knew about rockets, the launch blew me away (I use the phrase intentionally). The thrusters ignited, and even from afar I heard the engines roar and felt the ground quiver. A white plume formed around the launch site, from which, after few seconds, the space shuttle slowly emerged as it lifted off and cleared the launch tower. It accelerated upward, gradually rolled to its final course, and jettisoned its twin solid rocket boosters, roaring and shaking all the while. It was a spectacular experience. Out of sight, the craft continued to burn its liquid propellant and then dropped the external fuel tank before reaching its regular orbit beyond Earth's gravity. The launch succeeded.

The Gravity of the Status Quo

Projects fail for many reasons—poor problem definition, too many delays, budget shortfalls, and miscommunication, just to name a few. But one that is often overlooked is rooted in the project's launch itself.

New projects are like rockets: many forces oppose successful launches, and there must be enough thrust to take off. In undertaking a project, the greatest force to overcome is what I call the gravity of the status quo: a natural force that, by default, keeps a project grounded. Call it what you will—the way things are, the existing state of affairs, old habits, "we've always done it this way"—the status quo is a force to be reckoned with.

It's much easier to leave things the way there are than to move them toward a new state. Your team may be content, your cash flow stable, and your anxiety nonexistent, but you are going nowhere. New-ton's First Law of Motion states that an object at rest will stay at rest unless an outside force acts upon it.[3] Sir Newton, who first published this maxim in 1687, may as well have been referring to your next pro-ject: it will not move unless you supply enough force, that is, enough force to overcome the gravity of the status quo.

Launch Log: William's Woes

One of William's first job assignments after graduate school was a gov-ernment study on local infrastructure. His engineering firm had just been awarded the contract for a one-year phase, with the option to ex-tend the contact to future phases if the firm's performance was satis-factory. William was excited at the opportunity to add some govern-ment work to his portfolio, and he knew he had some project-specific technical skills that his team and client would value.

New to his job, William's learning curve was already steep, and this particular study made it even more precipitous. His calculations required both rigor and speed, a difficult combination for any engi-neer. Just when William thought he had crested a hill, the ground shifted and he fell behind. The whole project seemed to be a moving target. William soon became frustrated and demotivated, lost in the details, wondering why it felt so out of control. The problems seemed to worsen. He found that his colleagues, even those with more experi-ence, were struggling with the same project. William logged extra hours, hoping that throwing extra time at his tasks would help rein in the intractable project. With the firm's reputation and lucrative future work at stake, William knew he must do his best. But it seemed hope-less. "Are all projects like this?" he wondered. "Am I even making a difference?" William contemplated speaking out or even quitting his job, but he wanted to demonstrate his loyalty—and value—and secure his position in the firm. He didn't know, in Shakespeare's words,

> Whether 'tis nobler in the mind to suffer
> The slings and arrows of outrageous fortune,
> Or to take arms against a sea of troubles
> And by opposing end them.[4]

The project ultimately took three years and exceeded the original budget, without even delivering the full package. William's firm lost face and the contract extension as the client awarded future work to a competitor.

Launch Log: Taylor's Trouble

After an important multi-firm project had begun, Taylor, a longtime midlevel employee of Eastridge Enterprises, was assigned to the team. The invitation thrilled her, as it was her first project that involved working with partner company Welby Labs in a neighboring state. Her project manager, Dan, outlined her duties, which included data analysis, documentation, and integrating Welby's results into the deliverables (final products). He explained how Taylor would communicate with Welby's team regularly. He provided a scope of work, Welby's team roster, and a list of her specific tasks. Taylor jumped in straightway.

She soon found, however, that Welby's team members—both male and female—were slow to respond to her calls and emails. When they did, it was often too little, too late. She had heard only good things about Welby Labs. Why was this so difficult? Taylor's other teammates at Eastridge, including Dan, didn't seem to have the same problem; they communicated easily with Welby. Dan continually pressed Taylor for progress and pointed to the tight schedule. Without the right input from Welby, Taylor fell behind. Even with Dan's help she was unable to provoke timely and sufficient responses from the external team. Feeling extreme pressure to perform, Taylor chose to forge ahead and resorted to some risky assumptions in order to catch up.

Months later, the client questioned the poor assumptions and held Dan responsible. The project fizzled out and Dan was transferred.

Launch Log: Peter's Plan

Peter, a project manager, and his team had just begun a sensational pilot project. For his company, it was a new client and a new service; if successful, it could lead them to a new, uncontested "blue ocean" where they could enjoy a significant first-mover advantage.[5] They prepared a comprehensive proposal with incredible detail about tasks, methods, and schedule. Peter's team and the client's executive team attended the launch. After his presentation, Peter got the green light and the project took off. It progressed quickly according to plan, and a few months later Peter delivered a positive progress report.

The client's response, however, was a galvanic shock. "We're very concerned about your report," the client said. "This isn't what we were expecting at this point, and we're not sure how you got here. Didn't we agree on a different approach? You should be much farther along by now."

"How could that be?" Peter wondered. "We've followed our plan exactly." Now, two-thirds through the project, these basic questions were just emerging. He later corrected the problem, but not without great expense to his firm and a delay of their entry into a market that was, by that time, quickly becoming saturated.

What Went Wrong?

Why did these apparently well-prepared projects flop?

At first William attributed his struggles to his newness on the job. But his more experienced colleagues felt frustrated too, so it must have been something else. William later realized that a common vision hadn't been established during the launch. The firm was doing what it had always done. The client had a vision, and William's firm had a vision, but they weren't the same. The client envisioned different goals than the firm did, which ultimately led to scope creep, delay, and frustration. Unfortunately they didn't catch on to the dissonance until well after launch, when it was very difficult to correct course. And all along, William lacked his own purpose, not knowing if or how his daily work was contributing, or why he was contributing at all.

One might initially attribute Taylor's obstacles to her poor communication, but that's merely a symptom. The problem, she later deduced, originated when she had been excluded from the launch meeting, whether intentionally or not. The launch meeting was a critical event where workers from both companies met each other and formed a joint project-specific team focused on a common goal. Taylor's absence at the meeting simply perpetuated the status quo when Taylor had never worked with Welby before. Taylor wasn't there, so, to the other team members, she wasn't part of the team and didn't merit their prompt attention.

What about Peter and his well-crafted plan? Peter later recalled that he hadn't fully explained his plan to the executives at the launch. Pressed for time, Peter had glossed over some important assumptions about the scope, approach, and schedule. The project was a new idea, but Peter had relied on his old habits. Not knowing otherwise, the client had expected a fundamentally different, complete deliverable by now so they could make strategic decisions for the next year. The plan hadn't been clearly communicated, and the client's executives hadn't fully bought into it.

In each case, the failure occurred during the launch when some aspect of the status quo was too strong to overcome. Yes, there were other problems, too, but they cascaded from a primary failure during the launch. Specifically, the projects failed to properly express a powerful vision, a team, and a plan—the three launch engines, as we'll learn in the next chapter.

Launch Lessons

- Many failed projects can be traced to poor launches.
- Certain problems are just symptoms or results of poor launches.
- A failed launch engine—vision, team, or plan—can wreck the whole project, directly or indirectly.
- A project must overcome the gravity of the status quo, a natural force that keeps things the way they are.

Action Items

Based on what I learned from this chapter, I will:

_____

_____

_____

_____

_____

NOTES

[1] Robert B. Sowby, ed., trans., *Johann Wolfgang von Goethe: Proverbs* (2014), 12.

[2] See "STS-91," NASA Space Shuttle Mission Archives, last modified November 23, 2007, http://www.nasa.gov/mission_pages/shuttle/shuttlemissions/archives/sts-91.html.

[3] Isaac Newton, *The Principia: Mathematical Principles of Natural Philosophy*, trans. I. Bernard Cohen and Anne Whitman (Berkeley, CA: University of California Press, 1999).

[4] William Shakespeare, *Hamlet, Prince of Denmark*, ed. David Bevington and David Scott Kastan (New York: Bantam Dell, 2005), 3.1.58–61.

[5] See Reneé Mauborgne and W. Chan Kim, *Blue Ocean Strategy* (Boston: Harvard Business Review Press, 2005); Marvin B. Lieberman and David B. Montgomery, "First-Mover Advantages," *Strategic Management Journal* 9 (Summer 1988): 41–58.

Chapter 3

What Powers a
Successful Launch?

We shall not cease from exploration
And the end of all our exploring
Will be to arrive where we started
And know the place for the first time.

T. S. ELIOT[1]

Time was of the essence. In 1957, the Soviets were the first to launch a satellite, Sputnik, into Earth orbit. In April 1961, just months after President John F. Kennedy's inauguration, the United States botched the Bay of Pigs invasion in Cuba, and the Soviets achieved a second and more important space victory when cosmonaut Yuri Gagarin became the first human to journey into outer space.

That was enough. America needed a boost, and the Kennedy administration proposed a project that would be as risky as it was inspiring: to have the first human visit a celestial body beyond Earth. The Cold War was warming up, and recent events only spurred Kennedy's urgency to one-up the Soviets in the ultimate race to the moon.

The Moon Shot of the 1960s was one of the most audacious projects ever undertaken. Given all that was at stake and the effort it would require, Kennedy knew that the country needed a powerful launch.

Moon or Bust

In 1961 and 1962, Kennedy delivered two rousing speeches, one to Congress and the other to a crowd at Rice University. Excellent specimens of launch speeches, both illustrate Kennedy's conviction about the project's importance in terms of America's national security, scientific discovery, and world leadership. As you read these excerpts, pay attention to how well he addresses the vision, team, and plan so necessary for what would eventually become the Apollo program and place a man on the moon.

First, the speech before Congress on "urgent national needs" mere weeks after Gagarin's flight:

> Finally, if we are to win the battle that is now going on around the world between freedom and tyranny, the dramatic achievements in space which occurred in recent weeks should have made clear to us all, as did the Sputnik in 1957, the impact of this adventure on the minds of men everywhere, who are attempting to make a determination of which road they should take. ... Now it is time to take longer strides—time for a great new American enterprise—time for this nation to take a clearly leading role in space achievement, which in many ways may hold the key to our future on Earth.

What Powers a Successful Launch?

I believe that this nation should commit itself to achieving the goal, before this decade is out, of landing a man on the moon and returning him safely to the earth. No single space project in this period will be more impressive to mankind, or more important for the long-range exploration of space; and none will be so difficult or expensive to accomplish. We propose to accelerate the development of the appropriate lunar space craft. We propose to develop alternate liquid and solid fuel boosters, much larger than any now being developed, until certain which is superior. We propose additional funds for other engine development and for unmanned explorations. ... But in a very real sense, it will not be one man going to the moon—if we make this judgment affirmatively, it will be an entire nation. For all of us must work to put him there.[2]

Once Congress was convinced, Kennedy had to sell the idea to the populace, which was the purpose of his Rice address the following autumn:

For the eyes of the world now look into space, to the moon and to the planets beyond, and we have vowed that we shall not see it governed by a hostile flag of conquest, but by a banner of freedom and peace. We have vowed that we shall not see space filled with weapons of mass destruction, but with instruments of knowledge and understanding. ...

But why, some say, the moon? Why choose this as our goal? And they may well ask why climb the highest mountain? Why, 35 years ago, fly the Atlantic? Why does Rice play Texas?

We choose to go to the moon! We choose to go to the moon in this decade and do the other things, not because they are easy, but because they are hard, because that goal will serve to organize and measure the best of our energies and skills, because that challenge is one that we are willing to accept, one we are unwilling to postpone, and one which we intend to win. ...

But if I were to say, my fellow citizens, that we shall send to the moon, 240,000 miles away from the control station in Houston, a giant rocket more than 300 feet tall, the length of this football field, made of new metal alloys, some of which have not yet been invented, capable of standing heat and stresses several times more than have ever been experienced, fitted together with a precision better than the finest watch, carrying all the equipment needed for propulsion, guidance, control, communications, food and survival, on an untried mission, to an unknown celestial body, and then return it safely to earth, re-entering the atmosphere at speeds of over 25,000 miles per hour, causing heat about half that of the temperature of the sun ... and do all this, and do it right, and do it first before this decade is out—then we must be bold. ...

Many years ago the great British explorer George Mallory, who was to die on Mount Everest, was asked why did he want to climb it. He said, "Because it is there."

Well, space is there, and we're going to climb it, and the moon and the planets are there, and new hopes for knowledge and peace are there. And, therefore, as we set sail we ask God's blessing on the most hazardous and dangerous and greatest adventure on which man has ever embarked.[3]

Kennedy's moon speech at Rice University, Sept. 12, 1962.

What Powers a Successful Launch?

Kennedy's moon speeches were effective because they employed, according to one observer, "a transcendent rhetoric that utilizes three major strategies: a characterization of space as a beckoning frontier; an articulation of time that locates the endeavor within a historical moment of urgency and plausibility; and a final, cumulative strategy that invites audience members to live up to their pioneering heritage by going to the moon."[4] It's irresistible. The most well-known line, "We choose to go to the moon," earned a thunderous ovation.

On July 20, 1969, Apollo 11's lunar lander, the *Eagle*, touched down in the moon's Sea of Tranquility. Neil Armstrong, after stepping onto the lunar surface, broadcasted the now-famous line, "That's one small step for a man, one giant leap for mankind." The whole world was watching. Most people old enough to have witnessed the event via television or radio can recall exactly where they were and what they were doing at the time.

The following spring, after Apollo 12's successful landing, Apollo 13, commanded by Captain Jim Lovell, embarked for the country's third moon landing. It was the most famous moon mission that didn't land on the moon. (I knew all about it from Lovell's book *Lost Moon* and Ron Howard's 1995 film *Apollo 13*, based on Lovell's book. As a kid, I saw the film in the theater at least seven times and nearly memorized the script after it was released on home video.) Fifty-six hours into the flight, an internal explosion severely crippled the spacecraft and the three-man crew was nearly stranded in space. Thanks to round-the-clock work by NASA and other experts, the crew returned safely to Earth, and the mission was called a "successful failure."

In 2010 I shook hands with Lovell after he spoke at Brigham Young University, where I was an engineering student. To hear Lovell describe his Apollo 13 experience and meet him in person (though I was expecting Tom Hanks) was a special occasion for me. Even though I was familiar with the story, meeting a man who had lived it added a new, deeper perspective. He had actually been out there, drifting almost a quarter million miles from Earth, freezing in a damaged spaceship, unsure if he would ever return. But he did.

Four more successful Apollo missions followed through 1972. President Kennedy was long gone by then (assassinated in 1963) and unfortunately never witnessed the results, but his vision, team, and plan, articulated so clearly and so powerfully, had endured. To this day, only the United States has ever landed a man on the moon.

The Launch Engines

Now we come to the heart of the matter. In Chapter 2 we learned about three failed projects and the failed launches behind them. Here, we introduce the three launch engines that drive successful ones.[5]

In my career I've led or attended scores of launches, or kickoff meetings, in business, church, engineering, artistic, and academic settings. Some have been for small, brief, in-house projects; others have been for large, multi-partner, multi-year programs. Through my own experience and my interaction with many project managers, I have observed that, regardless of size or setting, the most successful launches address a trio of big-picture components: a *vision*, a *team*, and a *plan*. I call these the launch engines, which every project needs in order to overcome the gravity of the status quo.

Like a rocket, the launch sets the trajectory for the entire project. Yes, you can make in-flight course corrections, but most of the momentum comes from the initial thrust. If you burn the three main engines long enough during launch, you'll get off the ground and have enough momentum to propel you through the rest of the project.

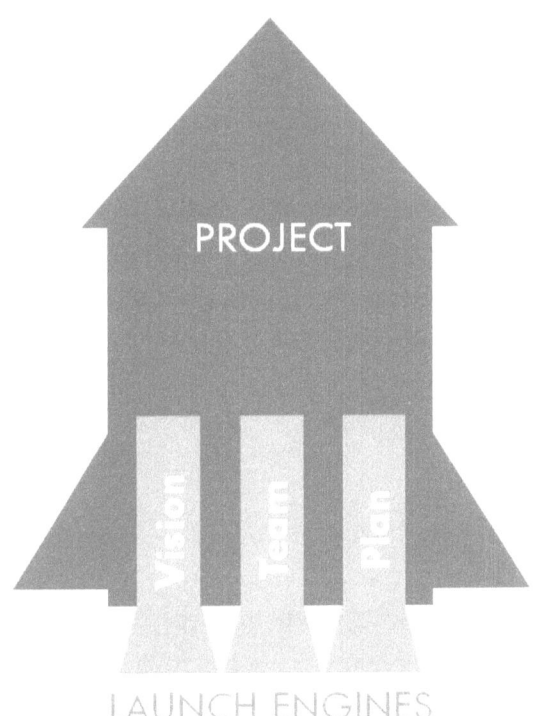

The three launch engines.

Years ago, under the direction of the now-retired John Miller, I performed with the American Fork High School Marching Band. That's a project too. I was the drumline section leader, and for three summers I worked with other band students to produce visually and sonically spectacular field shows for fall competitions in and beyond my home state of Utah. The group was a local aberration, an unusual concentration of musical passion in an otherwise fameless small town.

The band had a vision: to build champions and to build character. The band had a team: some 200 students and staff in any given year, plus a devoted network of parents, alumni, administrators, civic leaders, and other supporters. The band had a plan: practice. A lot. All

31

right, it was more elaborate than that—specific repertoire and formations, specific drills and rehearsal techniques, and specific practice schedules and deadlines—but we certainly put in the effort, rain or shine.

The launch engines were burning constantly, boosting the "supersize, uber-impressive, award-winning American Fork High School Marching Band" to become what is perhaps Utah's most decorated and most respected amateur musical ensemble.[6] The combination of an inspired vision and team, plus a plan to reach the goal, has made the band practically unbeatable.

Project Vision: Why

The process of inspiring others to act begins with *why*, a concept which leadership thinker Simon Sinek has studied extensively.[7] During the launch, you need to share your vision. Give people a reason to contribute to the project. Explain why you're doing it, why it's important, and why it aligns with organizational goals. An effective vision forms an emotional connection between the participants and the project, inspiring them to offer their best efforts and keep sight of their purpose when challenges arise. Chapter 4 discusses in more detail the project vision as a launch engine.

A project may be well planned and have a great team, but without a clear vision—a *why*—it is unlikely to succeed. William, the new graduate mired in the drawn-out government project, suffered from a lack of project vision, as did his colleagues. That engine failed. A proper launch with a deliberate vision would have helped them succeed.

In is moon speeches, President Kennedy engaged his audience by alluding to larger issues with phrases such as "the battle ... between freedom and tyranny," "the key to our future on Earth," and "new hopes for knowledge and peace." These concepts resonated deeply with

Americans at a time when Soviet conquest loomed and the United States needed a swift and conclusive Space Race victory. Kennedy envisioned an American moon landing not as a trophy stunt but as the very solution to these issues. His address to Congress address contains a project vision statement in the second paragraph: "This nation should commit itself to achieving the goal, before this decade is out, of landing a man on the moon and returning him safely to the Earth."

An inspiring vision unifies the project team and motivates them to perform for a cause that matters to them personally. Communicate it clearly at launch time and throughout the project. Steve Jobs said, "If you are working on something exciting that you really care about, you don't have to be pushed. The vision pulls you."[8]

Project Team: Who

No project goes anywhere without people. *Who* will fulfill the vision? Team members will be interacting with each other throughout the project, so it's important that they start off on the right foot together. Chapter 5 discusses the project team as a launch engine.

Taylor, the employee who struggled to communicate with Welby's personnel, was, to them, not part of the team. When Taylor was excluded from the launch meeting, they missed a critical opportunity to meet face to face, discuss how their roles complemented each other, and decide how their communication was to proceed. Taylor learned about the project only after the launch, and she felt like she was afterthought—whether she was or not—and Welby considered her just that. If she wasn't at the launch, her role must not have been critical. And if her role wasn't critical in the beginning, why would it be now? It all came secondhand. A proper introduction of the entire team could have avoided such problems and eased their cooperation.

A moon shot takes a team, and Kennedy chose the right one: the people of the United States. Even though only one person may physically visit the moon, Kennedy enlists the entire nation as the team, "for all of us must work to put him there." Kennedy considered the project a national priority and wanted every American to own its eventual success. His speech was designed, said one writer, "to convince the American people that they should shoulder the burdens, accept the risks, and reap the rewards of this adventure."[9]

Launch is the time to discuss and understand everyone's roles, as well as to catalyze the longer process of team cohesion. As Henry Ford said, "Coming together is a beginning; keeping together is progress; working together is success."[10]

Project Plan: What, How, When, and How Much

Now that you know why you're doing the project and who's involved, the project plan defines the remaining details: *what, how,* and *when.* There's also the issue of budget: *how much.* You've already charted the course in the planning phase, so now you can share it with the entire team and get consensus. Chapter 6 discusses the project plan as a launch engine.

Peter, the executive with the failed plan, should have clarified his plan and identified any discrepancies with his client early on. If time was short during the launch meeting, such an important item should have merited deliberate follow-up. Agreement on the plan—especially in this case, where the project was the first of its kind—should have been a prerequisite. A project without a plan may have the right people and a convincing destination, but little idea of how to proceed.

Kennedy's speeches outlined a plan of what, how, and when. We're going to the moon, of course, and that requires a serious rocket.[11] In contrast to the space shuttle I described earlier, which only orbited the Earth and never actually escaped the planet's gravity, the Apollo missions were bound for an extraterrestrial destination, farther than any previous manned flight, and consequently required much more thrust. The launch vehicle would be the Saturn V rocket, standing 363 feet tall—taller than the Statue of Liberty—and weighing 6.2 million pounds. At launch, it would produce more power than 85 Hoover Dams and deliver three astronauts and some 50 tons of spacecraft to the moon. Though not overly technical for a general audience, the main ingredients of an approach are there: develop suitable propulsion, thermally and structurally robust materials, and precise manufacturing techniques to build all the necessary systems for manned lunar space travel. Kennedy's timeline is also clear, with an ambitious goal to complete a moon mission by 1970. And he got the funding.

Plan-related problems can be avoided with proper attention during launch. In the words of time-management authority Alan Lakein, "Planning is bringing the future into the present so you can do something about it now."[12]

Launch Log: Walter's Website

An entry-level employee, Walter, had been studying the situation for some time: his company's website needed a makeover. The existing website was five years old but behaved like it was much older with an outdated design, obsolete technology, sparse content, and a clunky backend. He was no web guru or marketing expert, but Walter knew that the company could do better—and *must* do better in order to thrive. He envisioned a clean, simple, appealing website with quality content that would help market the company. The vision wasn't yet well formed, but it was enough to start.

When he raised the issue, Walter's managers suggested forming a website committee and, on the spot, appointed him to be its first chair. He was surprised but thrilled at the chance to lead. Though not part of his usual duties, this was Walter's first project management assignment.

Knowing he couldn't do it alone, Walter began selecting a team. He tapped Ted, the company's IT expert and a skilled web designer, to be the chief developer. He also recruited Jack, a company principal and proven advocate, to add some influence to the team. Finally, he invited the company's marketing director, Carly, to join the committee. Walter knew these people's skills and their interest in improving the company's weak online campaign. He had the right people.

The team met to outline the next steps. Walter shared his original vision of the website as a marketing tool, and his teammates suggested their own ideas about what the website should accomplish. Collaborating on a project vision helped the committee members own the project and feel committed. Though they never formalized a vision statement, it might have sounded like this: "Develop a website that advances our business through a strong online presence."

With a vision and team in place, Walter turned to preparing a project plan. Each team member had their own purposes for the website. Jack's goal was to increase traffic and recruit new employees. Carly wanted to share news and better advertise the firm's services and qualifications to prospective clients. Ted expressed a need to transmit large files and host clients' data. Walter wanted an engaging and easy-to-use website that would help grow the business. The team organized these ideas into four main objectives: Develop a website that allows us to market our services, share news, recruit employees, and host large files. These objectives defined the project's scope.

To define an approach, Walter consulted with Ted on the technical feasibility. They decided that a custom, responsive website built on a lightweight content management system would be best. Carly and Walter identified methods to develop new content, namely a portfolio, news area, and testimonials. Jack would liaise with management to ensure proper support and progress.

Finally, each team member estimated his required effort: Ted for design and programming, Walter and Carly for writing, and Jack for coordinating with management. The team settled on a budget and schedule compatible with their goals.

With the vision, team, and plan in place, the project took off. At almost every interaction, Walter checked the launch engines and made sure the project was still flying, even when some turbulence appeared or when minor course adjustments were necessary to correct assumptions and mistakes.

When additional website features were suggested, the committee judged them against the vision: Does this feature help us achieve our vision? Or is it a distraction? Features that didn't pass the test were rejected or postponed. Even when committee members disagreed on certain decisions, they agreed to remain loyal to the vision.

The team had united for a common cause during the launch and, despite differences of personality and agendas, continued to coalesce throughout the project. Walter soon spun off other projects with them: some workflow tools with Ted, a journal article with Jack, and an industry award with Carly. These interactions facilitated Walter's integration into the company as a trusted teammate and productive contributor.

The team's commitment to the project plan was essential. The objectives were clearly stated and often reviewed, the approach was informative, and the schedule pushed everyone to deliver on time.

After monitoring performance for six months after completion, the team concluded that their website redevelopment project had succeeded. The success, they realized, was due in large part to their rigorous devotion to vision, team, and plan during launch.

Applications

A strong vision, team, and plan propel a project. Any project. Even the best crime stories—a brilliant heist, for example—all share an exciting vision, team, and plan. Reflecting on the great variety described in Chapter 1, the launch engines apply equally to a yard sale as a moon mission. In either case you should ask yourself, "What's the vision? Who's my team? What's our plan?" Doing so will launch you on the right trajectory.

Launch Lessons

- Three launch engines—vision, team, and plan—power a successful launch.
- Vision addresses *why*, team addresses *who*, and plan addresses *what*, *how*, *when*, and *how much*.
- Projects take off when powerful visions, teams, and plans align.

Action Items

Based on what I learned from this chapter, I will:

_____

_____

_____

_____

_____

_____

NOTES

[1] T. S. Eliot, "Little Gidding" (no. 4 from "Four Quartets").

[2] John F. Kennedy, "Address to Joint Session of Congress" (speech, Washington, DC, May 25, 1961), John F. Kennedy Presidential Library and Museum, http://www.jfklibrary.org/Asset-Viewer/xzw1gaeeTES6khED14P1Iw.aspx.

[3] John F. Kennedy, "Address at Rice University on the Nation's Space Effort" (speech, Houston, TX, September 12, 1962), John F. Kennedy Presidential Library and Museum, http://www.jfklibrary.org/Asset-Viewer/MkATdOcdUo6X5uNHbmqm1Q.aspx.

[4] John W. Jordan, "Kennedy's Romantic Moon and Its Rhetorical Legacy for Space Exploration," *Rhetoric & Public Affairs* 6, no. 2 (2003), 210.

[5] The following content is similar to a stand-alone article I wrote for *Project Times*. Robert B. Sowby, "3 Keys to A Successful Project Kickoff," *Project Times*, May 24, 2016.

[6] Sharon Haddock, "John Miller to Retire After 30 Years of Successfully Leading AF Band to Victory," *Deseret News*, November 9, 2015.

[7] See Simon Sinek, *Start with Why: How Great Leaders Inspire Everyone to Take Action* (New York: Penguin, 2009). Also see Sinek's TED talk "How Great Leaders Inspire Action" (TEDxPuget Sound, September 2009), which is currently the third-most-popular TED talk of all time.

[8] Values.com, accessed July 20, 2016, http://www.values.com.

[9] Jordan, "Kennedy's Romantic Moon," 210.

[10] BrainyQuote, accessed July 20, 2016, http://www.brainyquote.com.

[11] The following facts come from "What Was the Saturn V?" NASA Knows!, September 17, 2010, http://www.nasa.gov/audience/forstudents/5-8/features/nasa-knows/what-was-the-saturn-v-58.html.

[12] BrainyQuote, accessed July 20, 2016, http://www.brainyquote.com.

Chapter 4

The Launch Engines:
Vision

*It's the possibility of having a dream come true
that makes life interesting.*

PAULO COELHO[1]

Taurus, a £500 million project to upgrade the London Stock Exchange from primitive paper-based trading to centralized computers, was to be a seamless, state-of-the-art, electronic system that would easily interface with other global systems and streamline international trading. The paper-based system, which origin-ated in the 1700s, was collapsing with the sheer volume of daily modern transactions as the market grew. Taurus would make trading more efficient, convenient, and reliable. Started in 1983, the project was staffed with experts, was well funded, was dutifully supervised, and would solve a definite problem. Taurus would revolutionize the securities industry and be its flagship project, leading the London Stock Exchange into the 21st century with an unprecedented fusion of finance and technology.

Yet even well into the project, there was no consensus on what Taurus would look like. The final features were unclear and uncertain, with ever-changing requirements dictated by numerous committees and stakeholders. As the scope expanded to 17 potential systems, attempts to merge and patch the scattered ideas created a sort of Frankenstein's monster. Some doubted whether the right technologies to drive such a complex service chain could even be acquired, tested, and implemented at all, let alone within the ambitious 18-month timeframe. Some brokers actually preferred paper certificates and fiercely opposed a technologically sophisticated replacement that would require fundamental changes to complex and well-established business processes. If you've ever struggled to learn a new computer program after several years on the job or were delayed at the doctor's office because "we just got a new system," you know how disruptive switching to a new technology can be. Five years in, the original Taurus design was scrapped in favor of purchasing and substantially modifying an existing system from the United States, which only increased complexity and delayed the rollout. "Further," said one study, "the confusion and unrealistic demand on delivery time grew as those responsible for delivery slipped into being unmotivated and skeptical about the prospect of any measure of success."[2] Deadlines are motivating, but only to a point. When the goal is not only vague but impossible, people find little reason to continue. The technical team often reported, "Yes, you are further forward but you are no nearer the end, because the end keeps moving."[3]

Taurus was suddenly abandoned in March 1993 when, after ten years of effort, it became apparent that it would *never* work. Investors didn't know whether to cheer or cry. By then, the stock exchange, local organizations, and registrars (trading middlemen) had sunk hundreds of millions of British pounds into a venture that was, in the end, utterly unsalvageable. "In theory it was marvelous; in practice it was a nightmare," wrote one commentator.[4]

The hazy direction, the kaleidoscopic demands, and the parties' inability to converge on a solution all sound much like poor William's case in Chapter 2, though on a grander, more public scale. Indeed, they share the same root problem: a lack of proper vision during launch and beyond. Analysis of Taurus's ignominious downfall revealed a number of contributing factors, including poor stakeholder management, underestimation of complexity, lack of effective governance, and poor decision making.[5] But, as one might suspect from the cases we've already studied, these were only superficial problems, mere symptoms of a more fundamental underlying failure: the project vision. Taurus was a dream, but, in Shakespeare's words, "a dream itself is but a shadow."[6]

As well intentioned as it may have been, Taurus's vision was poorly understood, demotivating, incredible (as in not credible), and challenging in the wrong way. The chilling conclusion: "If all project team members and stakeholders had a clear vision of the purpose of the project, Taurus's spectacular failure could have been avoided."[7]

Project Vision: *Why*

From the birth of Christianity to the founding of America to the fall of the Berlin Wall, vision has played a role throughout history. As one writer put it, vision "is a key you will find in almost every past or present example of significant human achievement."[8] While research on the impact of organizational visions is ubiquitous, the literature on project visions is sparse, though they are just as important within their own scope as organizational visions are in theirs.

The project vision then, not surprisingly, is the first and most important launch engine. It answers *why*, the essential starting point for inspiring action. "There are only two ways to influence human behavior," leadership thinker Simon Sinek said. "You can manipulate it or you can inspire it."[9] Manipulation is effective for achieving immediate results in the short run, but its effect wears off and its subjects wear down. Inspiration, on the other hand, takes more effort and patience but yields more sustainable performance. A vision gives project participants a reason for contributing. A vision clarifies the project's purpose, eliminates confusion, unifies the team, and inspires them to do their best, especially when difficulties arise.

A *project vision* is the picturing of the project's deliverables as the solution to the stated problem.[10] It's a preferred end state. Before you really start a project, you must have a firm idea of what it's all about. But more than a mental picture, it's a guide, a landmark, a lighthouse that both focuses your attention to stay the course and encourages you to press forward. While acknowledging that change is inevitable, the vision should be understood at the project's outset. The purpose of the project vision is to:

- Inspire and engage followers
- Create a bridge to the future
- Provide direction
- Establish standards
- Motivate leaders

Another illuminating definition comes from one of my neighbors and church leaders, David L. Kezerian. In his words, "A vision is an objective that inspires action." This comes from a man who was responsible for the spiritual welfare of thousands of people and who needed to regularly inspire church members to serve, teach, reach out, and live as true Christians. I like Kezerian's definition for its implicit emphasis on both faith (a goal or objective) and works (action): "For as the body without the spirit is dead, so faith without works is dead also," the Bible says.[11] C. S. Lewis captured this idea when he wrote that determining which is more important—faith or works—is like "asking which blade in a pair of scissors is most necessary."[12] Both are important, and one does not function without the other. Action without an objective is drudgery; an objective without action is dreaming. Together, they become a realized vision.

Beyond what I have personally observed, the management research supports visions not just in organizations but also in specific projects. One study found that "a significant driver of project management success is ... an inspiring vision of what the project is meant to achieve and how it can make a significant positive impact."[13] In another study of project leadership, researchers concluded that "the most significant success factor for project teams is that they have a common and shared idea of what difference they are trying to make as a result of the project."[14] This is exactly what a project vision is.

As a positive example, the Joint Information Management System (JIMS) began in the early 1990s to address the need for a central data repository for government agencies.[15] It was a complex undertaking requiring the cooperation of many stakeholders from four major organizations. Yet JIMS succeeded where other similar projects did not. The success "was substantially attributed to the project leadership group's use of a vision" that was maintained despite several setbacks.

The U.S. Marine Corps trains recruits to ask themselves and each other questions that begin with "why" when things are miserable.[16] "Why are you doing this? Why are you here?" Such questions help them link something difficult to a meaningful choice they care about, and that makes the task easier. Answers may be as personal and immediate as "To make a better life for my family" or as communal and transcendent as "To ensure that freedom endures." Either way, articulating *why* helps them connect emotionally to the task and frame it in the context of a vision much larger and more important.

The influence of your vision extends beyond the project team to those who will benefit from it: stakeholders, customers, and others who believe in your vision. "People don't buy *what* you do, they buy *why* you do it," Simon Sinek said.[17] This concept, Sinek argued, explains the success of the Wright Brothers, Martin Luther King, Jr., and Apple—all who, in the beginning, were competing against louder, richer, and more-qualified rivals attempting the same goals.

In Taurus we saw how a total lack of vision killed a project—a long, painful death from the inside out. Now what if there is a clear vision, but it doesn't catch on or is just dead wrong? Let's explore that variation.

When Marissa Mayer took over Yahoo as CEO in 2012, she candidly acknowledged how bad the situation was.[18] The internet company had been on a long losing streak, sinking from $7.2 billion in revenue to $4.2 billion in the previous four years. Employees were disheartened and the culture was stale. Mayer's simple solution to all this was to boldly proclaim her vision "to bring an iconic company back to greatness" through double-digit annual growth and eight other daring goals. The media loved this feminine paragon of willpower and leadership. Mayer, a Stanford graduate and one of Google's first employees, was going to turn Yahoo around.

By the end of 2016, Yahoo had lost another $4.4 billion, failed to achieve double-digit growth, compromised the personal data of 500 million users, and muffed all but two of Mayer's other goals. Boldness and confidence and willpower and positivity could not save Yahoo. Mayer's grand vision, her seemingly impossible "stretch goal," ended abruptly and quietly when Verizon agreed to take over the ailing company.

In the 1990s, Jim Collins and his colleagues introduced the idea of "big, hairy, audacious goals"—BHAGs, also called stretch goals—and the concept has been promulgated throughout the management literature and the business world with great success.[19] At Apple, Boeing, Google, GE, and other leading companies, stretch goals are inextricably tied to their culture of innovation. Stretch goals often attract the best people and create excitement to complete a project. But there is a dark side. Stretch goals can go too far, to the point of being unrealistic, demotivating employees, and encouraging undue risk-taking.[20] Yahoo's case shows that stretch goals alone do not magically transform a poor project or organization.

In what management researchers have called the "stretch goal paradox," organizations ill-suited to stretch goals misuse them (as Yahoo), and organizations that can benefit most from stretch goals seldom try them.[21] A condition of "desperately trying to avoid meltdown" is not conducive to stretch goals—that requires a different strategy. Instead, stretch goals are most effective in organizations that are thriving but complacent: ones with strong performance and unused resources. I am not discouraging BHAGs, stretch goals, and grand visions. (Kennedy's moon shot? Greatest BHAG ever.) They have proven to be very effective under the right circumstances. But they are a two-edged sword that must be wielded wisely.

As another example, consider J.C. Penney's 2011–2013 merchandising project, Fair and Square Every Day.[22] CEO Ron Johnson, a former Target and Apple executive brought in to reverse the iconic department store's bleak financial situation, proposed predictable "Every Day" prices to replace coupons and sales events, the store's longstanding revenue drivers. When I was a child, this is exactly how my mother shopped, and I remember accompanying her to our local J.C. Penney for the monthly sale whose deals she had dutifully studied in the Sunday paper. But under Johnson's direction, J.C. Penney adopted simpler price points, instituted color-coded price tags, and modified the entire pricing system that so many customers had become familiar with. Johnson also launched a fully revamped home department with brand-name merchandise like Martha Stewart in an effort to appeal to more-affluent consumers. Johnson's ambitious but risky plans were supposed to transform the century-old chain into the modern retail powerhouse he envisioned.

Like Taurus, the idea was appealing in theory but flopped in practice, as several business experts predicted it would. J.C. Penney's loyal customer base was accustomed to bargain hunting and thrilling sales, and the store's new "Every Day" pricing confused and bored these regular customers. Sales continued to slump as customers turned away and sought more exciting shopping experiences elsewhere. The project contributed to a $1 billion loss in 2012, and the company's final quarter that year has been called the worst in retail history.

In contrast to Taurus, which had a nebulous vision at best, Johnson's vision for J.C. Penney was lucid but ultimately didn't resonate with its most important stakeholders: loyal customers and the front-line staff who dealt with them. The Johnson era of "brand names sell" didn't work since most customers wanted to shop by price, not brand. The top-down approach of foisting a single person's vision on the rest of the project defies both the collaborative nature of project visions and the collective commitment needed to make them effective.

The cases of Taurus, Yahoo, and J.C. Penney illustrate how projects suffer from *no* vision or a *false* vision. But is the *right* vision enough by itself?

The 2016 U.S. presidential election was one of the most remarkable triumphs of vision I have seen. From the very beginning, outsider Donald Trump relentlessly targeted voters' discontent with what the political establishment, and the country, had become during the previous administration. He promised change as none other had dared to do: to return America to its former standing by focusing on its own affairs rather than those abroad and by shaking up the worn political structure. Trump's nationalist vision statement, "Make America Great Again," resonated so strongly with the electorate that they were willing to overlook flaws that would have doomed any other candidate: his lack of governing experience, his checkered business record, his cavalier geopolitical attitude, his poor debate performances, and of course his steady stream of impetuous and incendiary statements. Even with daily red flags, his campaign still succeeded. The day after the election, the *New York Times* reported the following:

> Donald Trump was right. Countless others were wrong.
>
> The pundits and pollsters who said the former reality TV star could not win the U.S. presidency, the Republicans who shunned him, the business leaders who denounced him and the Democrats who dismissed him failed to fully understand the depth of his support. ...
>
> "He was an imperfect candidate with a near-perfect message," said Ford O'Connell, a Republican strategist who has long backed Trump. "I don't think a lot of people understood that."[23]

Unable to offer much detail on *how* America could become great again or *who* would make it happen (besides himself), Trump focused on *why*. He won by articulating a vision many Americans shared. Trump's victory is a recent and prominent example of how a strong vision, a "near-perfect message," can make up for a lack of a plan and a team—at least initially. But I do know this: Trump's apparent success won't last without the right plan or team to back it up. It's certainly possible that Trump will rise to the occasion, that his cabinet will turn into a high-performing team, and that the new administration will craft policies to support his broad vision and lead America to greatness. Now that the election is over and Trump's presidency has begun, only time will tell if this unprecedented political experiment, a project with serious implications, will succeed or fail.

Vision Statement

A vision and a vision statement are separate but related concepts. The vision is a grand, encompassing idea with emotional weight; a vision statement is its linguistic representation—a concise, replicable declaration of the big picture, a sort of project scripture. It sets the direction and truly helps people see and understand. It is also distinct from a mission statement, which describes what an organization does.

Over a century ago, Henry Ford expressed his vision this way:

> I will build a motor car for the great multitude. It will be large enough for the family but small enough for the individual to run and care for. It will be constructed of the best materials, by the best men to be hired, after the simplest designs that modern engineering can devise. But it will be so low in price that no man making a good salary will be unable to own one—and enjoy with his family the blessing of hours of pleasure in God's great open spaces. [24]

Ford certainly achieved that and more, thanks in part to his ability to envision it and communicate it.

Advice on formulating an organizational vision statement is abundant. Here are a few basic principles that apply to project vision statements in particular: [25]

- **Simple**—Keep your project vision statement brief. (Organizational vision statements may be longer.) If it is longer than a sentence or two, it's not clear enough. This will facilitate communication and internalization. Try writing it on a business card.

- **Actionable**—Express the project vision with strong verbs like "deliver" or "produce" to encourage action.
- **Engaging**—Include concepts that will resonate with project participants and impel them to commit their best effort.
- **Collaborative**—Solicit input from all stakeholders, including your team and the client/sponsor. This will not only produce better ideas but will help them own and agree on the vision.
- **Forward-thinking**—Imagine the project's conclusion and express the vision in terms of the benefits and deliverables.
- **Specific**—If they are brief, you may mention a few key criteria or goals that will define success.

While you aim to articulate a clear vision from the very beginning, remember that your vision may evolve as the project unfolds and you learn more about the problem you are solving. If needed, rewrite your vision statement. And rewrite it again.

Consider the following examples of vision statements. In each case, the words were carefully chosen to capture the salient ideas and requirements:

- "Design an onboarding program that quickly transforms new employees into valuable long-term contributors."
- "Introduce a document management system that is flexible enough to be synchronized with other existing systems in the business."[26]
- "Establish and evolve department leadership anchored in teamwork and tools that drive transformative results and impacts."[27]
- "Develop a centralized case-tracking database system that avoids duplication, information entry errors, and wasted management effort."[28]

- "Prepare a prioritized list of low-cost engineering recommendations that guides the organization to more energy-efficient operations."
- "Inspire a consumer revolution that nurtures the health of the next seven generations."[29]
- "Take to market a copier that is small, inexpensive, and reliable enough for personal use on a secretary's desk."[30]

Notice how these examples follow a pattern:

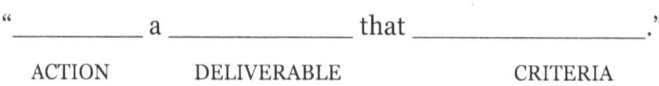

This pattern works well, but there are certainly other variations. Feel free to experiment and find your own. Every project and team is unique, so craft a vision statement that works for you.

A word of warning: As great as a vision statement is, it doesn't substitute for a detailed project plan. Your vision statement can't possibly include all the goals, expectations, criteria, descriptions, and definitions necessary for the project, and though it refers to a few, it doesn't define them concretely. In the first example above, how "quickly" is quickly enough to onboard a new employee? How is his or her "value" defined and measured? What does it mean to be a "long-term contributor?" These criteria must be defined more carefully elsewhere, usually in the project plan (Chapter 6). The vision statement is only useful when participants grasp the underlying details and the vision statement itself is just a symbol or reminder.

One of the best project vision statements I've seen is "Denver to Honolulu on a hot day." That may mean nothing to you, as it did to me the first time I encountered it. Allow me to explain. Aerospace company Boeing undertook its 777 program with very specific objectives about a new airplane's specifications and capabilities.[31] Following the format above, their vision statement may have read, "Manufacture a technologically advanced midsize commercial aircraft that strongly positions the company for the 21st century." But the exact specifications were too many to list, though a vision statement was crucial. Alan Mulally, the 777 program's general manager, simplified it with this beguiling phrase: "Denver to Honolulu on a hot day." To the project team, it was obvious: deliver an airplane with high-altitude capacity ("Denver") and extended operations ("Honolulu") to be ready by summer ("hot day"). What's more, the phrase was visual—you can imagine the flight—and engaging.

I recommend the following steps when creating a project vision statement:

- Form a small committee, perhaps three members, to oversee the development of a project vision statement. Avoid writing it alone; you should consult at least one other person as a reality check. Much will hinge on the statement, so it deserves proper attention.

- Interview key stakeholders about what they think the project should accomplish. Ask them to describe the deliverables and the key criteria it must satisfy. What does success look like?

- Draft a project vision statement. Remember to make it simple, actionable, engaging, collaborative, forward-thinking, and specific. You may use the format presented above or develop one that better suits your project.

- Share your draft with key stakeholders and team members and solicit feedback. (Avoid J.C. Penney's top-down approach.)

- Revise the draft and produce a final project vision statement. You may not satisfy everyone, but do your best to settle on a reasonable product.

Formally present the project vision during the launch (discussed among other launch procedures in Chapter 7). Start with the project vision statement and discuss the meaning and purpose of each term. This is like a set of building blocks that make up a structure, where participants should begin to build their own understanding of the vision.

Internalizing the Vision

A vision is useless if not communicated, understood, and adopted by every team member. Not everyone in William's firm or the Taurus team understood what they were doing and why they were doing it. Perhaps some did, but the vision didn't pervade the entire team. The engine ignites when everyone commits; a common vision binds a team together and inspires them to do their best.

Each team member must internalize the vision. Memorizing the vision statement is one option (hence the recommendation for brevity), but beyond memorization, each team member should be able to articulate the vision in his or her own words. It goes beyond motivation—you must arouse passion, an emotional connection to the project.[32] Team members must personally identify with it and understand how they are expected to contribute. It must be meaningful to them in their own way for their own role. They should ask, "What does it mean for me?" and "What's my role in fulfilling the vision?" John Kotter, an emeritus Harvard Business School professor and noted management thinker, said that you must be able to "communicate the vision to someone in five minutes or less and get a reaction that signifies both understanding and interest."[33]

Once formed and introduced during the launch, the vision must be reinforced regularly if it is to be internalized. Even multiple speeches and email blasts are insufficient since they constitute only a small portion of the project team's communication volume.[34] More frequent and diverse exposure is needed. Mulally's maxim "Denver to Honolulu on a hot day" was made into a pinback button with a cartoon he had drawn; employees wore the button to remind them why the project existed and why they were contributing.

A pinback button for Boeing's 777 project featuring Mulally's cartoon.

Consider the following ideas to help you and your team internalize the vision:

- Make vision the first item on every project meeting agenda.
- Share the vision through multiple communication channels: speech, email, social media, video, etc.
- Include the vision statement in presentations, memos, and other project-specific document templates.
- Design posters, banners, or signs with the vision statement and post them in conspicuous locations around your workplace.
- Reinforce the vision in routine day-to-day interactions with your team members. Gauge how well they understand it. When questions arise, link your responses to the vision.
- Demonstrate your own commitment to the vision by your words and, more importantly, actions.

Note that these suggestions, while presented here in the context of project-specific visions, also work for organizational visions.

Visualization and Vision

Athletes, musicians, astronauts, and other high performers are often coached on how to visualize their ideal performance.[35] American Fork's marching band was no exception, and many of our rehearsals began with this very exercise: imagining a flawless show in terms of one's maneuvers, breathing, and musicality—even before we had learned the music or formations. The intent is that visualization of the future will stimulate action in the present that will enable achievement of the ideal. Visualization translates vision into action.

While they envision the outcome, high performers know that they win not at the end, but *now*. This is my poem "The Winning Field," composed during my marching band years:

> Underneath the stadium lights
> The champion's games are done,
> But long before those crowning fights
> He has already won.
>
> On other fields, far, far away,
> With coaches and with teams,
> The champion struggles every day
> To win within his dreams.
>
> Focused effort on those fields
> Is the champion's secret story;
> It's not the final game that yields
> The victory or glory.

For at least one of the Wright Brothers, the vision began long before he was really capable of achieving it: "Orville's first teacher in grade school, Ida Palmer, would remember him at his desk tinkering with bits of wood. Asked what he was up to, he told her he was making a machine of a kind that he and his brother were going to fly someday."[36]

Launch Log: Emma's Education

Emma was a bright undergraduate senior at a respected university in her home state. She earned decent grades, participated in student associations, and liked her major. Until her senior year she hadn't thought much about graduate school; she had been concentrating on her coursework and on finishing one degree before she considered starting another. Feeling somewhat burned out after a few years of studying, Emma wasn't quite ready to pursue further education. She assumed that, if she wanted, she could easily continue into the department's master's program like most of her peers.

One night she and a roommate, Rachel, were discussing their graduate school plans. "I'm going to stay here and earn a master's degree," Rachel said. "My department's graduate program is one of the best in the country, and I'd fit right in. What about you?" Emma admitted that since she hadn't really thought about it, she would probably do the same. "A lot of my classmates are doing it, and I guess it's convenient," Emma conceded. Rachel was surprised. "'Convenient?'" she retorted. "Since when have you done anything 'convenient,' Emma? You chose one of the hardest majors there is. And I've never known you to do something because 'everyone is doing it.' You're smart, you're hard working, and you deserve better. Don't settle for that if it's not what you want. So what *do* you want?"

Emma thought. "Well, it would be cool to go to a prestigious school, like Stanford or Princeton or Yale," she said. "I think they have really strong graduate programs in my field. I visited some of them when I was a kid and dreamed of studying there." She paused. "But it's just that—a dream, Rachel. I'd never make it in. It's too competitive. I don't have perfect grades or great recommendations, and our university here probably isn't even on their map. No, Rachel, it's not for me."

Rachel persisted. "It's not too late. You'll never know if you don't try. And why shouldn't you try? You've got one year left here. You could work hard to boost you GPA. You could take on a research assistantship so you could get to know a professor who can recommend you. And you can stand out in other ways, like scoring high on the GRE. I've seen how passionate you are about your field. Show them that. You could totally do it, Emma. It wouldn't be as easy as staying here, but it would be better."

Rachel was right, Emma thought. Why not? After exploring Yale's graduate programs, Emma decided she wanted to apply. She chose a few backups just in case, but she envisioned herself at Yale. Rather than knowing a Yale graduate, she would *be* a Yale graduate, one of the top researchers in her field who could go anywhere and do anything. But first she needed to act on her vision.

Emma committed herself to improving her grades. She knew it would require sacrifice, and when she woke at 4 a.m. to finish assignments, when she attended extra lab sessions to get help from the tutors, and when she declined dates and outings in order to catch up, she had to remind herself why she was doing it. (Rachel reminded her, too.) Emma's vision guided everything she did and inspired her to give it her best. Emma studied diligently for the GRE, purchasing official practice exams and study materials. She knew other Yale applicants would score above the 95th percentile, so she had to be there, too. When her first exam score wasn't high enough, the poor college student groaned and paid out another $160 and did it all over again until she got a near-perfect score. To secure a set of strong recommendations, she began a research project with two professors in her department. Emma did so well with her research, in fact, that the professors begged her to stay and offered her a full-ride scholarship and generous stipend if she were to go straight into their doctoral program, skipping over the master's degree. Emma turned them down. It was attractive, no doubt, but it wasn't consistent with her vision. (They still recommended her.) With solid grades, a high GRE score, excellent recommendations, and a passionate vision, Emma submitted her applications in the spring.

A month later, she was accepted to her second-choice graduate school and was invited for a campus visit. Emma had just completed a full day of faculty interviews, research presentations, and lab tours intended to win her over. Her faculty host was very persuasive. This isn't bad, Emma thought—at least as a backup.

Just as she was leaving, Emma checked her smartphone for any messages—a regular practice in these suspenseful days, waiting to hear just how much her life could change. At the top of her inbox was an email from the Yale University admissions office. Her eyes bulged but she kept calm. Emma read it quickly and turned to her host.

"It's been a wonderful visit, professor, and I'm very impressed. But I'm sorry I won't be attending your school after all," she explained. She held up her smartphone. "I've just been admitted to Yale."

Launch Lessons

- The first launch engine, project vision, is a guiding force that inspires action. It is the picturing of the project's deliverables as the solution to a stated problem.

- The vision statement is a concise linguistic representation of the actual vision.
- Successful launches require that every team member adopt and internalize the vision in their own way.
- Visualization is a tool that translates vision into action.

Action Items

Based on what I learned from this chapter, I will:

_____

_____

_____

_____

_____

_____

NOTES

[1] Paulo Coelho, *The Alchemist*, trans. Alan R. Clark (London: HarperCollins, 2002), 11.

[2] Dale Christenson and Derek H. T. Walker, "Understanding the Role of 'Vision' in Project Success," *Project Management Journal* 35, no. 3 (September 2004), 46.

[3] Helga Drummond, "Riding a Tiger: Some Lessons of Taurus," *Management Decision* 36, no. 3 (1998): 143. The article's title refers to the proverb, "He who rides a tiger can never get off."

[4] Hamish McRae, "Comment: Taking the Bull by the Horns," *The Independent*, March 11, 1993.

[5] "London Stock Exchange – Taurus," Catalogue of Catastrophe, International Project Leadership Academy, September 14, 2012.

[6] William Shakespeare, *Hamlet, Prince of Denmark*, ed. David Bevington and David Scott Kastan (New York: Bantam Dell, 2005), 2.2.260.

[7] Christenson and Walker, "Understanding the Role," 46.

[8] James P. Lewis, *Working Together: 12 Principles for Achieving Excellence in Managing Projects, Teams, and Organizations* (Washington, DC: Beard Books, 2002), 41.

[9] Simon Sinek, *Start with Why: How Great Leaders Inspire Everyone to Take Action* (New York: Penguin, 2009), 17.

[10] R. Max Wideman, *Wideman Comparative Glossary of Project Management Terms*, s.v. "project vision," http://www.maxwideman.com/pmglossary.

[11] James 2:26 (King James Version).

[12] C. S. Lewis, *Mere Christianity* (New York: HarperCollins, 2001), 148–149.

[13] Christenson and Walker, "Understanding the Role," 39.

[14] Wendy Briner, Colin Hastings, and Michael Geddess, *Project Leadership* (Aldershot, UK: Gower, 1996), 89.

[15] Details about this case are drawn from Christenson and Walker, "Understanding the Role," 46–48.

[16] Charles Duhigg, *Smarter Faster Better: The Secrets of Being Productive in Life and Business* (New York: Random House, 2016), 29–30, 272–73.

[17] Sinek, *Start with Why*, 41.

[18] Facts about Mayer and Yahoo come from Forbes, "The World's 100 Most Powerful Women"; Jon Swartz and Mike Snider, "Marissa Mayer's Diminishing Legacy at Yahoo," *USA Today*, October 18, 2016; and Sim B. Sitkin, C. Chet Miller, and Kelly E. See, "The Stretch Goal Paradox," *Harvard Business Review*, January–February 2017.

[19] See, for example, James C. Collins and Jerry I. Porras, *Built to Last: Successful Habits of Visionary Companies* (New York: HarperCollins, 1994); Jim Collins, *Good to Great: Why Some Companies Make the Leap ... and Others Don't* (New York: HarperCollins, 2001); and Sitkin et al., "The Stretch Goal Paradox."

[20] See, for example, Daniel Markovitz, "The Folly of Stretch Goals," *Harvard Business Review*, April 20, 2012.

[21] Sitkin et al., "The Stretch Goal Paradox"; Sim B. Sitkin, C. Chet Miller, Kelly E. See, Michael Lawless, and Andrew Carton, "The Paradox of Stretch Goals: Organizations in Pursuit of the Seemingly Impossible," *Academy of Management Review* 36, no. 3 (July 2011): 544–566.

[22] Details about this case are drawn from Kim Bhasin, "Failed J.C. Penney CEO's Vision Still Sinking Company Long After His Departure," *Huffington Post*, July 17, 2013; Rafi Mohammed, "Understanding J.C. Penney's Risky New Pricing Strategy," *Harvard*

Business Review, January 30, 2012; "J.C. Penney," Catalogue of Catastrophe, International Project Leadership Academy, July 28, 2013.

[23] "How Trump Crushed Naysayers with a Coalition of the Forgotten," *New York Times*, November 9, 2016.

[24] Roger Burlingame, *Henry Ford: A Great Life in Brief* (New York: Knopf, 1954), 62.

[25] The first three points were adapted from Ian MacMillan and Rita McGrath, "Corporate Ventures: Maximising Gains," *Financial Times* (London), *Mastering Management*, October 16, 2000.

[26] Eric McConnel, "Project Vision Statement," *MyMG*, November 12, 2010.

[27] Adapted from Park City Municipal Corporation, *Water and Energy Conservation Program Management Plan*, December 2016 draft.

[28] Based on the information given in the article, this is what I think JIMS' vision statement could have looked like. Christenson and Walker, "Understanding the Role," 46–47.

[29] Seventh Generation, "Mission + Action," accessed January 27, 2017, https://www.seventhgeneration.com/mission.

[30] MacMillan and McGrath, "Corporate Ventures." The statement describes one of Canon's products.

[31] Lewis, *Working Together*, 46–50.

[32] Lewis, *Working Together*, 42.

[33] John P. Kotter, "Leading Change: Why Transformation Efforts Fail," *Harvard Business Review*, January 2007.

[34] Kotter, "Leading Change."

[35] Stephen R. Covey, *The 7 Habits of Highly Effective People: Powerful Lessons in Personal Change* (New York: Free Press, 1989), 134; Daniel McGinn, "The Science of Pep Talks," *Harvard Business Review*, July/August 2017. Also see Craig Manning, *The Fearless Mind: 5 Essential Steps to Higher Performance* (Springville, UT: CFI, 2009).

[36] David McCullough, *The Wright Brothers* (New York: Simon & Shuster, 2015), 1.

Chapter 5

The Launch Engines:
Team

Thee lift me, and I'll lift thee,
And we'll both ascend together.

JOHN GREENLEAF WHITTIER[1]

W hen I was 17, my father and I took a short hike to the American Fork Twin Peaks, the highest point in Salt Lake County, Utah. We hiked a lot back then—about 200 miles per year—but this one was special: it marked the completion of our quest to reach the highest peak in each of Utah's 29 counties. It also signified the end of driving nearly 5,000 miles and hiking 183 miles to reach the goal my father, my brother Craig, and I had set three years before.

One spring a series of articles about hiking the highest peaks in each county in Utah appeared in the *Salt Lake Tribune* Outdoors section, and soon Craig brought home the accompanying guidebook.[2] After some initial study and discussion, the three of us decided that we would like to start our own adventure to visit each of the peaks. We figured it would take about 20 "weekend warrior" trips over four summers. We called ourselves the Sowby Summit Team.

When we began, I had been on a few Boy Scout hikes and backpacking trips, but my 14-year-old body wasn't used to hiking a lot. My father, however, was an accomplished runner and had no trouble staying fit and pacing himself on long backcountry adventures; Craig was an amateur cyclist and climber in good physical condition. I'm sure I whined a lot on those early hikes: "I'm hot." "I'm tired." "My feet hurt." "Are we there yet?" I wasn't much of a contributor at first, but more of a drag. I couldn't drive or set up a tent or read topographic maps, so I relied on my father and brother for most everything besides the actual hiking. I enjoyed the mountains and going on these "man trips" with my dad and brother, but I just didn't have the skills to be a great mountaineer. But my teammates knew that I had potential, that I could improve, and that I wanted to be part of the journey.

Our team logo, which we affixed to gear, maps, and car bumpers.

Over time I developed the necessary skills and grew stronger. My legs got used to rugged terrain. My heart and lungs acclimatized to high altitudes. My back became accustomed to heavy loads. (My marching band regimen—probably the most physically demanding project I had undertaken up to that point in my life, dashing around a football field with 45-pound drums for hundreds of hours—also boosted my fitness.) I learned how to drive, set up a tent, read maps, build fires, tie knots, avoid sunburn, and find my way in the wilderness. I learned how rivers, glaciers, and faults had shaped the wild landscapes I traversed. I studied the habits and habitats of goats, picas, and other mountain creatures. Through these and other activities I earned numerous Boy Scout merit badges leading to an Eagle Scout award. As my outdoor skills improved, I took on more responsibilities in the Sowby Summit Team, planning the trips and leading the hikes. We soon developed a rhythm and became a well-functioning team as we bagged one peak after another.

Every trip was memorable—some for the wrong reasons. We endured six hours of rain and hail while descending Kings Peak—Utah's highest summit, at 13,534 feet—in the Uinta Mountains. One hike, near the Nevada border, was just plain ugly. Another required 600 miles of driving and only 4 miles of hiking, an all-day event starting at 3 a.m. But by and large the experience was positive. We did all this because we liked to be in the mountains, enjoyed challenges, wanted to see more of Utah, and liked to spend time together. Further, our team had committed to a goal. When the going got tough, we reminded each other of our vision to set foot on each county's highest peak. We were a great team, and we succeeded.

Soon after finishing our 29 peaks tour, Craig and I climbed bigger mountains: the Grand Teton in Wyoming (via the Owen-Spalding route) and Mt. Whitney in California (via the mountaineer's route), the highest peak in the continental United States—both of which would have been impossible for me just a couple years before. Craig later summited Mt. Rainier in Washington and scaled the 1,500-foot face of Angels Landing in Utah's Zion National Park. I volunteered with the Timpanogos Emergency Response Team for several seasons, helping hikers on one of Utah's most popular mountains and making some 20 or 30 ascents in just a few years.

The Sowby Summit Team has continued to evolve over the years. Craig is now training his own children to hike, in the Appalachian Mountains. My father, now 72, still hikes with me, though his pace is (just a bit) slower than it once was. Our team often reflects on those mountain experiences that shaped us.

Project Team: *Who*

Who will fulfill your project vision? It may be you alone—an individual enterprise—though even an undisclosed solo project relies on some outside support or some past work by someone else. ("If I have seen further, it is by standing on the shoulders of giants," Sir Isaac Newton said.[3]) More likely, however, you will need help from other individuals committed to your same purpose. Either way, your project needs a *team*. At the very least, it could be you plus a friend or spouse. At the most, it could be an entire organization or country. A proper team— one uniquely qualified and that can share your vision—is the second launch engine.

The amount of literature on teams—their behavior, challenges, and performance—is enormous. From sports to business to military, there is no shortage of documentation about what works and what doesn't. For now, let's return to the basics.

What is a team? In their seminal research on high-performing teams, Jon R. Katzenbach and Douglas K. Smith offered this defini- tion: "A team is a small number of people with complementary skills who are committed to a common purpose, set of performance goals, and approach for which they hold themselves mutually accountable."[4] All five ingredients are necessary. The common purpose, of course, is the vision, which they must in some way own, or at least shape, in order to succeed. Performance goals, articulated in the project plan, challenge and inspire the individual members, requiring them to work together. The approach, also part of the project plan, tells how the team will reach its goals. The skills must be complementary and often develop over time; most teams don't possess all the necessary skills at first. (Team development is discussed in Chapter 8.)

Above all, mutual accountability is what distinguishes teams from working groups: without it, they perform as individuals; with it, they become a powerful unit of collective performance. This mutual accountability must emerge naturally from within in the group, which can be difficult since the usual pattern of organizational life biases us toward competition and individualism rather than trust and commitment. Each team member must be accountable to and for each other if the team is to succeed. This is related to the concept of psychological safety, which Harvard Business School professor Amy Edmondson described as "a team climate characterized by interpersonal trust and mutual respect."[5]

Let me offer a few examples. Highland Rugby of Salt Lake City can claim the most unique win/loss record in its sport: 419 wins and 10 losses between 1976 and 2012, including 19 USA Rugby national championships in the 26 years the championship existed. That kind of performance doesn't just happen. Larry Gelwix, who coached the team during this extraordinary 35-year period, understood what a team is and what it requires, as the 2008 film *Forever Strong* depicts. Gelwix said that great achievements are never totally attributable to one person, but rather that a number of individuals each play an indispensable part. One of his most well-known "Gelwixisms" captures the mutual accountability that successful teams must have: "It doesn't matter *who* scores, it matters that *we* score."[6]

John Miller, my high school band director, knew this, as did his students. "Miller said if there's a secret to coming away with the first-place trophies year after year, it's in convincing the kids they matter. ... 'They learn to work as a team.'"[7] We understood mutual accountability. If one person played a wrong note or stepped out of formation, it affected the entire band, like a weak link in a chain. One time a few students deliberately stayed too long on a lunch break in order to miss part of the afternoon rehearsal. But rather than start without them, we waited. When the sluffers returned, they had intended to slip in unnoticed; instead, 200 band students and staff were standing waiting for them in the parking lot. One by one, each latecomer had to apologize to the entire band for his poor decision and for letting down his team. Only then could our rehearsal resume, which was extended minute-for-minute beyond the usual time to make up for the delay. Many of us missed carpools or family dinner or church activities as a consequence of the actions of a few. But that was the price of membership. We had committed to the same goals and we needed each other. American Fork band members knew what it meant to be mutually accountable.

A few years ago I taught an engineering course at Salt Lake Community College. It was a new project for me, and though I had a vision and a plan, I didn't get to choose my team. The students chose me—perhaps because I was the only choice they had. Nine strangers would spend four months under my tutelage as a means to satisfy a graduation requirement. How could I manage a group of students I didn't even know? By considering them as a team and holding them accountable for everyone's learning. I included this statement in my syllabus:

We are a community of learners. The choice to enroll in the class is yours. Once you enroll, however, you are committed. As a member of our learning community, you commit to:

- Come prepared for each class, ready to learn and participate
- Complete assignments on time (this allows prompt feedback, helps class members, and maintains schedule)
- Make me aware of topics or questions you would like to discuss
- Provide feedback so I can improve your learning experience
- Take responsibility for your own learning and help others do the same

As instructor, I commit to:

- Come prepared for each class
- Create meaningful learning experiences
- Offer prompt, valuable feedback on your work
- Help you meet your academic and professional goals

I look forward to working with you this semester.

When I shared my vision and introduced the syllabus on the first day of class, the students had neither questions nor qualms about what was expected of them. They were thrilled, in fact, that I cared enough to make them commit to each other. They knew I was committing just as much as they were. We were a team of learners.

Teaching those students was a delight. Their curiosity and their naïveté, their humor and their wisdom were inimitable. Did they always submit assignments on time? No. Was my grading always prompt? No. Did we have fun and learn a lot together? Yes—and the rest doesn't really matter. Even when we slipped, the mutual accountability we each felt inspired us to help each other and try harder next time. On the last day of class, each student shook my hand before departing and said how much they had enjoyed the journey. "This has been one of my favorite classes," one said. "Thank you so much. We'll remember you forever."

Choosing a Team

Project teams, like projects themselves, come in many varieties. A project team usually operates with the following roles:

- **Client/sponsor**—The client/sponsor is a high-level leader in the sponsoring organization who defines the project's goals, allocates resources, communicates with stakeholders, makes business decisions, and is accountable for the project's outcome. He promotes the project throughout his or her organization. For in-house projects, this is usually a senior executive. For consulting projects, this is a high-level official in the client organization. The client/sponsor guides the work but is mostly external to the project team.

- **Project manager**—With the client/sponsor, the project manager defines the scope, budget, and schedule and develops an approach to deliver the project. She chooses team members and assigns tasks. She oversees daily progress and reinforces the vision. She ensures that goals are met on time and on budget. The project manager may fill other roles such as motivator, negotiator, mentor, evaluator, mediator, and exemplar. She must also do her fair share of the work to build trust. *Learn to Launch* assumes that you are the project manager.

- **Team members**—Team members are individual contributors with technical, social, and organizational skills relevant to the project. They complete individual deliverables and collaborate with others to meet the project goals.

First, you must select a proper team; not just anyone will do. As Jim Collins's seminal study observed, people are *not* your most important asset—the *right* people are.[8] How do you know who is right? Above all, team members should share your project vision. This seems obvious, but I've seen some project managers choose team members based on other factors like popularity, availability, or affordability. Ultimately, those who embrace the vision will produce better results than those who are passively assigned to a project or who have exceptional skills but simply aren't committed. Even someone with meager skills will find a way to contribute to a project he believes in. Sharing the vision and evaluating the interest it generates should be your first approach to selecting an effective team.

After that, your team needs a blend of technical, social, and organizational skills, plus a good scoop of energy and enthusiasm. You must decide which recipe of teammates best produces the desired blend. Consider the project's scope and what skills are needed to match each task. Talk to peers and other project managers to get recommendations. You're not likely to get all the capacity you need at first. Certain skills will need to develop over time, so select willing-to-learn team members and plan for some training to occur. Attitude and personality matter a lot, too.[9] Given a choice between a savvy but jaded team member and one who is less qualified but excited to participate, I'll take the latter. Look beyond technical skills to see who is well connected, can offer resources, is confident, or has a unifying influence.

As a young consulting engineer my technical skills were average. I was surrounded by engineers, so I didn't always stand out. But after a while my peers and project managers realized that I excelled at writing reports, giving presentations, and communicating with clients—and that I *liked* these tasks. (My double major in liberal arts was a good choice after all.) I was often selected for project teams for these reasons and worked alongside more technically proficient engineers who contributed in their own ways. My technical skills continued to develop, of course, and even though I was officially an engineer, my role was much broader as I took on communicative and organizational tasks on behalf of the team. A team's strength lies in its set of complementary skills.

A client, Dave, once shared with me his philosophy on selecting engineering consultants. "I surround myself with the best consultants in each field," he told me one day after a launch meeting. "Other people like one-stop shopping. Not me. I choose the best team for the job each time. Honestly, I would never hire your firm to do X, but you're really good at Y. So every time Y comes up, I'll choose you." This surprised me because I hadn't thought about strengths and weaknesses in that way. For Dave, my firm was one of several team members. We didn't have all the expertise he needed for everything all the time, but we had exactly what he needed at certain times. This is the power of a project team.

Sometimes the team is larger than you think. My wife, Christie, and I recently visited the United Kingdom, where Christie spoke at a global music conference. We approached our trip like a project: we had a vision, we were a team, and we planned carefully. While traveling, however, I realized that our "team" was more than just the two of us. Other important team members included Delta Air Lines, ScotRail, Staffa Tours, Transport for London, InterContinental Hotels Group, and several other businesses that helped us complete a successful trip. While these external team members didn't know of our exact plans and vision, they provided the expertise we needed and were committed to helping customers have a satisfying travel experience, so that's why we chose them. Our trip would not have succeeded without them. This illustrates how organizations themselves can be external team members to help you accomplish what you intend to do. Just as we had a choice of hotels and airlines overseas, you may have a choice of software, banking services, or equipment that will influence the project's outcome. Gauge how critical these decisions are and choose the *right* team members to help you succeed.

Talent Alone

"Oh, that was *beautiful!*" they tell Christie after a concert, crowding her to one side of the stage. "You're so talented." She's a professional classical pianist, a Doctor of Musical Arts, and an experienced piano educator. She is satisfied with her performance and graciously accepts the compliment.

The "talent" compliment is appreciated. It's even true. But, more importantly, it's incomplete. Yes, Christie is talented. But she also works hard and has help: 12 years of university education, 23 years of practice, and a lifelong team of teachers, family members, and friends. Christie, like most successful professionals, realizes that talent alone is insufficient. "There comes a time," she told me once, "when you find that your own talent is not enough. You need to work hard and learn from others to go beyond what you are capable of on your own. You need a team."

Now consider the 2004 U.S. Olympic men's basketball team. Up to that point, previous U.S. teams with Michael Jordan and Shaquille O'Neal had dominated the Olympics with a 24–0 record. In 2004, the lineup was equally talented, with names like Duncan, Wade, James, Iverson, and Marbury. But it was a haphazard team, assembled just weeks before the Games. Their performance was a disappointing flop. They simply couldn't perform together. Team USA suffered its largest loss in Olympic competition and sputtered to a bronze medal behind Argentina and Italy.

Clearly, they had talent, but that wasn't enough. Talent is just one ingredient in a complex and shifting team recipe. An overdose of talent can't compensate for a lack of vision, chemistry, commitment, or tenacity.

The story of the 1980 Olympic U.S. hockey team coached by Herb Brooks is just the opposite. Brooks's vision statement might have been, "Develop a team that can defeat the Soviets." The Soviets were the four-time defending Olympic champions, professional athletes who had played together for years and formed the most formidable team on ice. At the tryouts, Brooks addressed a motley group of college athletes he didn't know and who had never played together before. Brooks, however, understood that a team is more than a group of talented individuals. "Gentlemen, you don't have enough talent to win on talent alone," he tells them, as portrayed in the 2004 film *Miracle*. "All-star teams fail because they rely solely on the individual's talent. The Soviets win because they take that talent and use it inside a system that's designed for the betterment of the team. My goal is to beat 'em at their own game." Brooks knew that talent is necessary but not sufficient, and he applied that talent to get the team to improve together. It worked: The U.S. team ousted the Soviets in the semifinals and secured a gold medal for the United States, a welcome win in the heart of the Cold War.

Human performance scientist Craig Manning, who coached Christie on performance skills for several years, tells a related story in his book *The Fearless Mind*.[10] Manning coached women's tennis at Brigham Young University. On the first day of practice one season, he and his assistant observed the two newest players. One woman, whom he calls Hailey, was strong, trained, fluid, and explosive, with desirable modern topspin strokes. She was physically gifted and had great serves and volleys. The other new athlete, whom he calls Olivia, was lanky and slow, with spin-less strokes at least ten years out of date. After watching, Manning and his assistant agreed that at least one of the two could help the team, referring to Hailey. And they wondered if they had made a mistake in inviting the less-talented Olivia onto the team.

Fast forward a few years and the outcome is entirely different:

> Despite our early observations about Olivia's lack of physical talent, she was very coachable. She did everything we asked her to do. But even more important, it seemed like we would teach her something once, and we wouldn't have to teach her that specific skill again. As coaches we were able to move forward onto other more advanced skill sets at an accelerated rate. Over time Olivia was able to take what physical skills she had and magnify her strengths, leveraging her potential to heights I never expected.

She finished her senior year as the team's number-one player, ranked 16th nationally, and became one of the winningest tennis players in BYU history.

It's not that Christie, Olivia, and Brooks's hockey players weren't talented. They were. But more importantly, they learned from coaches and others how to leverage their strengths, overcome weaknesses, and produce high performance.

At Launch Time

Though informal planning meetings have already occurred, launch is the time to formally acquaint everyone on the project team who will be involved, whether core or peripheral. The *HBR Guide to Project Management* says that "being together at the beginning of their long journey and getting to know one another on a personal level will build commitment and bolster participants' sense that this team and project are important."[11] I couldn't agree more.

An all-hands launch meeting or kickoff meeting (discussed more fully in Chapter 7) is the opportunity to bring everyone together. If physically gathering all team members is infeasible, at least have them virtually participate by video or phone. The launch meeting should be designed around your team and empowering them to begin working on the project. Ask team members to introduce themselves, describe their backgrounds and skills, and explain how they will contribute. Also mention other stakeholders not present—customers, the board, or the public, perhaps—and describe how they could influence the project. During the meeting, establish an expectation of collaboration. You might include a specific teambuilding activity to break the ice and get to know each other. Encourage participants to ask questions, voice concerns, and share ideas. After the meeting, allow some time to continue conversations informally so team members feel comfortable with each other.

Even for small projects, a launch meeting of appropriate scale is invaluable. I've worked on small, local projects where I wasn't invited to the in-town launch meeting because the budget supposedly didn't allow it. I ended up doing 90 percent of the work, but I was never sure what the project was about or whom I was dealing with. Instead, I either bombarded my project manager with petty questions that would not have been necessary had I attended, or else I guessed poorly about how to proceed and had to repeat some work, both which threatened to drain the budget anyway. It would have been better to have everyone attend the launch meeting and clarify the expectations up front, regardless of the project's size or budget.

Developing a productive team takes time; the group must advance through the necessary and inevitable stages of forming, storming, norming, and performing.[12] Still, the mutual accountability so necessary for teams should start growing as soon as possible. Goethe said,

> The smallest garden plot will flourish
> When one knows well how to nourish.[13]

Make it easy for team members to meet, bond, and begin advancing together toward a shared objective. Your efforts during launch should produce fertile ground and provide initial nourishment for the roots of team performance.

Launch Log: Roger's Rally

In one consulting project, Roger had worked with the client, Debbie, on other projects and had met with her several times to define the scope and objectives of the new project. But Roger didn't know the rest of Debbie's staff. These people were her boots on the ground, the team members Roger and his colleagues would work with for the next six months and whose insight was critical to the project's success. Conversely, they hadn't met Roger's team, and knew little about the project or his firm.

Fortunately, Roger recognized this obstacle. He and Debbie agreed that a project of this nature required the total integration of both teams to facilitate communication, decision making, and rapid progress. Working as two disconnected teams, with Debbie and Roger being the only point of contact, was not an option. Debbie described her employees and their roles to Roger, and Roger proposed which of his people would be a good match to contribute complementary skills. Roger then pitched the project to his colleagues and invited, rather than assigned, them to participate. Debbie did the same, explaining how the two organizations were to work together as one team.

The launch meeting was held at Debbie's office. She and her staff were there to greet Roger's consulting crew as they filed in, and Roger made sure that everyone sat interspersed around the table so as to avoid a "face-off." Both teams, historically separate, now rallied around the same table, forming a new project team committed to a common goal. After Debbie presented the vision, the participants introduced themselves and discussed how each would contribute to a positive outcome. They identified external stakeholders and established a communication plan to facilitate information sharing. Roger then introduced the project plan and welcomed comments and questions. Thirty minutes of networking were built in to the launch meeting so the team could begin to become acquainted and start working together.

The team's introductions and interactions during the launch set the tone for their collaboration thereafter: they felt comfortable as a project team, knowing each other and being committed to the same purpose. The early emphasis on team development led to a successful project.

Launch Lessons

- The second launch engine is the *right* team.
- When choosing team members, their interest in the vision matters more than their skills or experience.
- Being together when starting a project helps team members build relationships and commit to the journey.
- Avoid all-star teams that rely too much on individual talent and that lack mutual accountability.
- Teams need time to develop. Use the launch to catalyze the process.

Action Items

Based on what I learned from this chapter, I will:

_____

_____

_____

_____

_____

_____

NOTES

[1] While I can't confirm the exact source, this Quaker proverb, of which there are many variations in syntax and punctuation, is often attributed to Whittier.

[2] The *Salt Lake Tribune* series and the guidebook *Hiking Utah's Summits* (Falcon Guides, 1997) were written by Paula Huff and Tom Wharton. After bagging all the peaks ourselves, I responded with my own article describing our experience: Robert Sowby, "Climbing Utah—All of It," *Salt Lake Tribune*, September 16, 2004.

[3] Isaac Newton, letter to Robert Hooke, February 5, 1676. The idea originates from the 12th century, but Newton's expression is the most familiar.

[4] Jon R. Katzenbach and Douglas K. Smith, "The Discipline of Teams," *Harvard Business Review*, March 1993.

[5] Charles Duhigg, "What Google Learned from Its Quest to Build the Perfect Team," *New York Times Magazine*, February 25, 2016.

[6] Doug Robinson, "Larry Gelwix the Real 'Forever Strong' Coach," *Deseret News*, October 7, 2008.

[7] Sharon Haddock, "John Miller to Retire After 30 Years of Successfully Leading AF Band to Victory," *Deseret News*, November 9, 2015.

[8] Jim Collins, *Good to Great* (New York: HarperCollins, 2001), 51.

[9] See, for example, Dave Winsborough and Thomas Chamorro-Prmuzic, "Great Teams Are About Personalities, Not Just Skills," *Harvard Business Review*, January 25, 2017; Charles Duhigg, *Smarter Faster Better: The Secrets of Being Productive in Life*

and Business (New York: Random House, 2016); Charles Duhigg, "What Google Learned."

[10] Craig Manning, *The Fearless Mind: 5 Essential Steps to Higher Performance* (Springville, UT: CFI, 2009), 62–63.

[11] Harvard Business Review, *HBR Guide to Project Management* (Boston: Harvard Business Review Press, 2012), 102.

[12] See Bruce W. Tuckman, "Developmental Sequence in Small Groups," *Psychological Bulletin* 63, no. 6 (June 1965): 384–399.

[13] Robert B. Sowby, ed., trans., *Johann Wolfgang von Goethe: Proverbs* (2014), 19.

Chapter 6

The Launch Engines:
Plan

Our goals can only be reached through a vehicle of a plan, in which we must fervently believe, and upon which we must vigorously act. There is no other route to success.

PABLO PICASSO[1]

One of my favorite sports is ultimate frisbee, a non-contact team sport in which points are scored for passing the disc (frisbee) into the opposing end zone. A player may not run with the disc; it may only be moved by passing while the player maintains a pivot point. An incomplete or out-of-bounds pass is a turnover to the opposing team. During possession, teammates maneuver about the field to stage a series of incremental passes that advance the disc toward the end zone.

In one particular match, I was playing with a mix of experienced and novice players. An experienced teammate observed that the novices on my team didn't have the awareness, timing, or technique to throw or catch even short passes. Every time they attempted a pass, it was intercepted or fumbled. Our team was suffering, unable to approach the end zone.

Instead, my teammate proposed, the novices should through throw the disc as far as they could toward the end zone. It was unlikely to be caught by a teammate and would result in a turnover, but at least it would be going farther in the right direction. And chances were that the opposing team, which also had novices, would fumble within one or two short passes and the possession would return to us, and we'd be that much closer to scoring than we would have had we tried to complete short, conservative passes in a single possession. In other words, since we didn't know exactly how we would arrive in the end zone, we needed to first move the disc within striking distance, even if we gave up a turn in doing so. We would be trading accuracy for distance, but once near the end zone, our experienced players could execute a few short passes to score.

I was intrigued. Would it really work? It defied my prior ultimate experience, but that wasn't helping us now anyway, so we agreed to try it. A few minutes later with a few points to our credit, I had to admit that our unusual strategy was working. It was leading us in the right direction.

Charting the Course

With the vision and team established, you're ready to ignite the final launch engine: the project plan. It answers the remaining questions of *what*, *how*, *when*, and *how much*.

The Launch Engines: Plan

Before launching, you'll need to chart the course—the path that will lead you and your team to your vision. Just like in ultimate frisbee, you probably won't know exactly how to get there—most projects involve unpredictable paths with numerous turns, decisions, and detours along the way—but you need enough of an idea to set you in the right direction.

Since you can't predict exactly how your project will unfold, charting the course means that you plan to head in the right direction with some major choices. If I were driving from Salt Lake City to Boston and had no map, I would start driving east on Interstate 80 and figure out the rest later. I know Boston is east of Salt Lake City, so that's the direction I would go. In fact, if I stayed on Interstate 80, it would take me all the way to New York City, which is just a few hours from Boston, and I could finalize my route from there. Even the well-planned Apollo flights needed manual course adjustments when approaching the moon, after the Saturn V rocket delivered them most of the way.

Since many project details are unknown at this point, you need a general strategy, like in my ultimate match, that is both clear enough for immediate action and responsive enough for unpredictable execution. You've already developed a vision and chosen a team. Questions to ask when charting the course include:

- What are the main tasks that will get us closer to the goal? What will make the most difference?
- How will we complete those tasks? What's our approach?
- When should the entire project be complete? What are the milestones?
- How much will it cost? What time, money, technology, and other resources do we have?

These ideas should form part of your project plan, which will evolve and grow as new information arises and decisions are made during the project. Course corrections—the finishing touches—will come later. The point is to make a rough first attempt at getting close to the objective, and then refine the plan from there. If available, review the debriefing notes from your last project (more on debriefing in Chapter 8).

Getting Started

The project plan usually takes the form of a written document or charter. Depending on your preferences and the project's complexity, it might be a single printed document, several digital documents, or a website. I'll offer some general guidance, but remember that the format, organization, and content of your project plan are at your discretion.

The project plan, not surprisingly, should begin with the project vision statement. In fact, all planning should stem from the project vision. For now, just write the vision statement at the top of your document. Later on, it may appear on a cover page below the project title or as a tagline on a website.

The next step is to clarify and define the vision statement in detail. In Chapter 4, for example, we saw the vision statement "Design an onboarding program that quickly transforms new employees into valuable long-term contributors." It's a good vision statement—brief, actionable, and forward-thinking. It states an objective and a few criteria that begin to describe what the project should accomplish. But it's too vague to work with on its own. What does it really mean? How "quickly" is quickly enough? One month? One year? Who qualifies as a "new employee"? A recent graduate? An internal promotion? An older, experienced executive new to the company? What "transformation" are we referring to? How do we assess the new employee's value and contributions? How long is "long-term," and why does it matter?

The vision statement is helpful, but it needs further clarification in the project plan. Each of the questions should be answered with input from key stakeholders as well as the client/sponsor. In this case, one might propose the following definitions that will clarify whether the project to design the onboarding program has been successful:

- "Quickly"—within six months; beyond passive or natural growth; accelerates break-even time (when value produced exceeds value consumed); implies regular feedback and interaction; may require training and other professional development; early intervention and remediation in case of problems.
- "Transform"—acknowledges a change of state, a process of development; requires deliberate action and input of resources.
- "New employees"—new hires, interns, promotions to new positions, etc., regardless of age or experience.
- "Valuable"—provides solutions; works efficiently; helpful and knowledgeable; billable (individual goals to be defined by management).
- "Long-term"—loyal to company; shares company values; sustainable; satisfied with job; has potential for at least five years' employment.
- "Contributor"—team player who supports the business with unique skills; receives positive performance evaluations from teammates; doesn't impede others' performance; improves capabilities of company.

While such definitions could continue indefinitely, you must dissect the vision statement enough to ensure that each part is readily understood and that the statement can remind team members of the more precise language and the broader vision.

Next, develop a project understanding. This is a statement of one to three paragraphs that summarizes why the project exists, what you know about it, and what is to be done. As a consultant I like to include the organization's vision or mission statement to show that I understand how the project aligns with their values. Here's an example from an engineering project:

> We understand that the water utility needs a high-level review to identify energy efficiency opportunities and recommend further steps to manage its energy use. This fits with its recently launched efforts in master planning, system inventorying, and asset management. We will analyze the water distribution system and identify energy-saving opportunities to help fulfill the utility's mission "to supply high-quality water, at a reasonable cost, while conserving water resources for future generations."

You might also describe what data are available, what past efforts have accomplished, and what resources can be deployed.

After the project understanding, you're ready to write the scope.

Scope: *What*

The scope, or statement of work, is the *what*: a suite of tasks designed to meet the overall objectives. It specifies the size of the effort, what is—and isn't—included, and how tasks are structured. You've probably discussed the scope informally with the client/sponsor, other stakeholders, and team members already, but now it's time to make it official.

The scope itself is best presented in outline or bullet form, and each task contains a few basic elements: its name, objective, input, activities, output (deliverables), and assumptions. It might look like this:

TASK 2: ENERGY BASELINE DEVELOPMENT

Objective: Develop energy baseline against which future energy performance can be measured.

Input:

- List of facilities and locations.
- Monthly facility-level energy use and cost data.
- Staff input on planning priorities.

Activities:

- Meet with staff to discuss planning priorities.
- Compute monthly energy intensities for each facility and the system as a whole.
- Prepare graphs of monthly values to identify seasonal patterns.
- Prepare maps to identify spatial patterns.
- Prepare baseline report.
- Meet with staff to discuss findings and future work.

Output:

- Energy baseline report.

Assumptions:

- System contains 17 facilities.
- Client will provide data within 30 days.
- Scope includes two on-site meetings of one hour each.
- One hard copy and one PDF copy of the report will be provided.

The objective states what the task should accomplish and how it will be used. The input section describes what information is necessary to complete the task. The activities section presents a sequence of smaller tasks designed to meet the objective. The output section indicates what deliverables, if any, will result. For all elements, the level of detail with each task will depend on the project.

The assumptions section is critical for further defining the scope boundaries. In considering your assumptions, ask yourself, "What has to be true for this scope, budget, and schedule to work?" If the water system actually has 40 facilities instead of the assumed 17, that threatens the budget or schedule. If the client takes too long to provide data, the project won't finish on time. More than two on-site meetings could overrun the budget. Delivering ten hard copies takes more effort than one. Writing assumptions into the scope helps protect you from blowing your budget or schedule. It also prevents scope creep (see Chapter 8).

Do not confuse the project's purpose with its scope, and don't let your client/sponsor confuse them either. This happened to me once with a client who thought that my team would provide all the necessary information to run an agency grant program when we were really just delivering the first phase. A project's purpose is the general benefit it will provide, while the scope is what the project team commits to complete toward fulfilling that purpose. It's good to think about the big picture, but you might only be painting part of it. You can always deliver more later if you want to, but don't bite off more than you can chew.

You must define what the project includes and what it doesn't, and then you must clearly communicate and regularly monitor those sharp boundaries. Failing to define, communicate, and control the scope is like signing a blank check: you give someone else permission to spend as much of your money (or time) as they want.

The project team and key stakeholders should understand the scope before the project begins. I've encountered several situations where this didn't happen. Partway through the project, the client expects one thing, but the project team delivers another, or the client thinks something is in the scope that really isn't. Resolving such problems is awkward since it usually requires telling the client that he's wrong and that he's not getting what he thought he was, or admitting that you failed to adequately communicate the scope and get his approval. It can also happen the other way around: the project team works on something they think is part of the project but is actually beyond the scope. While these problems are not impossible to overcome, it's better to share the scope with team members and stakeholders up front and get their consensus. It's your responsibility to ensure that everyone understands and accepts the scope.

For example, last July, in the middle of Utah's hot-and-dry season, my lawn sprinklers failed. I hired a professional, Joe, to fix them. It was an unexpected project with potentially serious repercussions. I, as the project sponsor, stated my scope and objective, plain and simple: "Please fix my sprinklers. I need to water my lawn." I didn't care how Joe did it, it just needed to happen soon. My scope defined the ends, but not the means—that's what the approach is for.

Approach: *How*

The approach, or method or means, is the *how*. As part of your project plan, it describes how you will complete the scope.

The tighter the budget or schedule or scope, the more innovative the approach must be. That's what makes the difference. If you're a manufacturer, you can't make the same product for less money on a faster schedule by using the same processes and equipment you always have. If you're a contractor competing on price for a fixed scope and schedule, you can't propose the same approach as other candidates. If you're a software developer aiming for rapid prototyping on a small budget, you can't use rigid or waterfall methods. In other words, if you want better performance, you can't rely on the same methods you've already used. You must differentiate your approach.

Questions to answer when considering the approach include:

- How will we gather information?
- What assumptions are we making? (What has to be true for our project to succeed?)
- How will we make decisions?
- How will we communicate?
- What processes, resources, and tools will help us succeed?
- What is unique, competitive, or valuable about our approach?

Seek your team's input on the approach before and during launch. Get everyone to agree, at least generally, on how they will complete the work. Avoid overprescribing at the individual level since everyone has their own work style and going against it could threaten performance and job satisfaction. Launch is the time to identify and resolve such issues. Describe the approach in your project plan so team members can refer to it later on.

Unlike the scope, which should be developed with significant input from the client/sponsor, the approach should be left to you to leverage your team's full experience, knowledge, and skill to fulfill the vision.[2] When repairing my sprinklers, I explained my scope but I left the approach to Joe. I didn't have the skills to fix my sprinklers—that's why I hired Joe in the first place—and even if I did, I wouldn't tell Joe how to do it. His choice of materials, tools, and techniques was almost trivial to me. I trusted his expertise and let him solve the problem with whatever approach he thought would give the best results—as long as it happened soon.

Schedule: *When*

The schedule is the *when*. As a piece of your project plan, it specifies deadlines for individual tasks as well as larger project milestones. A commitment to schedule encourages team members to work together for on-time project delivery.

There are many tools for drafting a schedule: time boxing, critical-path network diagrams, Gantt charts, and PERT charts.[3] The choice of tools is up to you. They all involve breaking down the scope into bite-size chunks and examining the relationships among tasks (e.g., Task A must finish before Task B can begin, but Task C can occur at the same time as Task B). What are the bottlenecks? Is there any slack? Is the workload balanced? Only after considering task relationships can you define an overall schedule.

The schedule must match the scope and the approach, and of course, the team. How long will it take to complete the proposed work with the resources you have? On one hand you might be too ambitious and propose a swift but fragile schedule that shatters with just one unexpected twinge. There will be times when this is necessary and you must take the risk. On the other hand you might be too conservative and propose a safe but sluggish schedule that misses the opportunity. This is also situationally appropriate and you'll have to accept it. Circumstances permitting, however, choose something in between: a reasonable and robust schedule that can withstand some interruptions while still fulfilling the purpose.

My sprinkler issue was urgent. The heat was over 100 degrees and my grass was scorched and dying. My yard looked awful, a prickly brown blemish in an otherwise beautifully landscaped neighborhood. I knew the homeowners association might crack down on me if I didn't fix it promptly. I chose the schedule: I wanted my irrigation restored within two days. Joe committed. The scope, approach, and schedule were settled. Now it was just a matter of money.

Budget: *How Much*

So far we've discussed the need for a scope, approach, and schedule. A fourth component surrounds them all: money. While I won't delve into the details of project budgeting here, I must acknowledge that budget is the critical factor in many projects. In the engineering consulting industry where I've spent most of my career, the budget matters. Staying within the budget on any given project is critical. Otherwise, the difference comes out of the firm's profits.

Your project plan should include a budget to accompany its scope, approach, and schedule. Consult with the client/sponsor and key team members to develop a draft budget; this way you get team buy-in and a reality check on your own estimates. During launch, present the budget and discuss what it means for each team member. Make sure everyone knows what the budget is, both in total and for their respective tasks. I find it best when everyone can be responsible for their own budget. It doesn't absolve you of your duty as project manager to monitor the budget, but it lets team members be mutually accountable for controlling it: no one can claim ignorance for blowing their part of the budget. This requires that the budget status be updated regularly and that team members can access budget reports and make decisions accordingly. You'll continue to monitor the budget throughout the project, but during launch everyone should at least be aware of it and commit to follow it.

When my sprinkler system failed, I risked losing my entire lawn and incurring the wrath of the homeowners association. I didn't have the skills to do it all myself, and it needed to be repaired right away. Although Joe's price quote caused some sticker shock, any other option would either take too long nor not solve the problem. I had no choice but to pay up if I wanted to keep my grass—and my good standing in the neighborhood.

A Balancing Act

It is often said that from among scope, schedule, and budget you may only choose two. Two are fixed, and the third must be flexible. This is called the triple constraint, the iron triangle, or the project management triangle.[4] You can have a comprehensive scope and a fast schedule, but it will be expensive. You can have a cheap but fast project, but you won't get as much. You can choose both comprehensive and inexpensive, but the project will take longer. Good, fast, or cheap? Choose two.

Let me offer a few examples. Last Christmas, Christie was in charge of a project to update and produce the family cookbook. The family wanted it to be a quality product (scope constraint) but still affordable (budget constraint). That meant Christie needed plenty of time (schedule variable). She asked herself, "How long to I need to produce a cheap but good cookbook?" Rather than hire an editor, she spent hours editing and formatting all the recipes herself. Rather than printing at a local print shop at ten cents per page, she opted for a more distant one at three cents per page, even though she would need time to travel there. Rather than taking the books to a bindery, she bought inexpensive spiral bindings and borrowed some binding equipment to do the job on her own. Her choices to spend more time were both necessary and deliberate since the scope and budget were fixed.

What if the scope and schedule are fixed, but the budget is unconstrained? In reality, few projects are like this; budget is usually the constraint. In an engineering project I was involved in, my firm helped the client, a city water utility, identify some water infrastructure needs. After discussing our recommendations, the city decided it wanted to construct the improvements (scope constraint) by the following summer (schedule constraint). Their question to us was, "We'll need to ask the city council for a bond to fund this project. How much will it cost?" With the budget defined from the prescribed scope and schedule, the city secured the funding and we completed the designs and oversaw the construction of a successful project.

In some projects, the budget and schedule are fixed and the scope is variable. Our trip to the United Kingdom, for example, had a specific time window and a finite budget. I had one week off work and had saved a few thousand dollars, plus tons of SkyMiles and hotel points. What could we do within those constraints? In addition to necessary transportation, lodging, and food for a one-week trip, we determined that our budget allowed for three castle tours, a Loch Lomond cruise, one BBC Scottish Symphony Orchestra concert, an excursion to the Hebrides Islands, one West End show, a Harry Potter tour, several museums, and souvenirs for ourselves and family members. We couldn't stay too long or spend too much, so we planned to do what was most important to us.

So far the tripartite scope–schedule–budget model makes sense and is very useful for defining project success. It works. But it's incomplete and therefore only *mostly* true: it ignores the role of the *approach*. If your approach is outstanding, you can overcome some of the traditional constraints.

Consider the Interstate 15 Corridor Expansion (I-15 CORE), Utah's largest transportation project and the fastest billion-dollar highway project in U.S. history.[5] The Utah Department of Transportation (UDOT) fixed a budget of $1.7 billion and a deadline of 36 months, with a *minimum* scope to improve 14 miles of highway. UDOT then invited competitive bidders to propose the best package: "What can you build in 36 months with $1.7 billion?"

After reviewing the proposals, UDOT selected and partnered with Provo River Constructors (a joint venture of Fluor Corporation, Ames Construction Co., Ralph L. Wadsworth Construction Co., and Wadsworth Brothers Construction Co.) to form a project team. The scope was massive. The project widened the freeway by two lanes in each direction for 24 miles (well beyond the minimum 14 miles), extended an express lane, replaced the original asphalt with high-performance concrete pavement, and rebuilt or replaced 63 bridges and 10 interchanges. The project was completed six weeks ahead of schedule and $260 million under budget. It received the 2013 Grand Prize in America's Transportation Awards and has been a model for major highway projects ever since.

But *how* did the I-15 CORE happen? The bidders knew that since the budget and schedule were constrained, they needed to propose a huge scope in order to be selected. But a huge scope means a gigantic budget or a long schedule—unless you change your approach. To deliver an ambitious scope, the team had to find ways to save money and time over a typical highway project. They couldn't propose the same standard methods and expect to win the bid, let alone succeed on the project. They needed to differentiate on approach.

The project team proposed and effectively employed several innovative techniques as part of their winning approach. As a project delivery method they selected design–build, meaning that the same team would both design and build the I-15 CORE, thereby shortening the schedule and improving workflow between traditionally separate engineering and construction firms. They researched interchange options and rebuilt interchanges following new, more efficient designs to improve traffic flow and safety, including some of the first diverging-diamond interchanges and continuous-flow intersections in the state.

They devised lane splits to divert traffic around center-of-highway work zones and confined most lane closures to overnight periods. They used wireless paving technologies and a concrete pavement with a 40-year design life. An extensive communications program informed the public of construction conditions and closures.

Most prominent of all, in a method called Accelerated Bridge Construction, they built bridges on the side of the freeway and then moved them into place overnight. Yes, you heard right. In 2011 when the Sam White Bridge was moved, I witnessed it in person with dozens of engineers from all over the world. The freeway closed for "one big night" to move one big bridge: a 354-foot span weighing almost 4 million pounds. It was the largest such move in the western hemisphere, happening right in my hometown of American Fork. I watched through the mist that chilly spring night as the bridge was lifted, rotated, and rolled into place on a remote-controlled transporter with hundreds of wheels, all within just a few hours. I drove under the bridge the next morning. "Well, *that* wasn't here yesterday," I said to myself. "But it didn't just walk over here on its own, now did it?"

The team's approach to the I-15 CORE may not have been part of the selection process, but it enabled them to offer more scope for the same price and schedule—a loophole in the iron triangle. My friend Todd Jensen, the I-15 CORE project director, called the approach "innovation at an unprecedented level to ensure we delivered this project in record-breaking time and under budget."

The Sam White Bridge rolled into its final location on Interstate 15 overnight.

Launch Log: Brandon's Blog

Among other responsibilities, Brandon oversaw his company's blog and social media. After examining the analytics to determine what content users most engaged and how often, Brandon decided that he needed to write a new blog post every two weeks. Anything more frequent didn't have time to reach enough users, and anything less frequent made the content seem stale. The marketing department agreed with Brandon's two-week recommendation.

He worked hard. He interviewed experts and conducted careful research. He wrote elaborate, lengthy pieces about company news, industry trends, and how-to articles. He published every two weeks—at least at first.

Soon Brandon's other responsibilities of meetings, data analysis, and presentations displaced his blogging projects. The marketing department wanted him to publish regularly as planned, but he simply couldn't keep up. Post intervals stretched to three weeks and then four as other demands competed for his time.

Brandon discussed the issue with his marketing co-worker Jill. She immediately recognized the problem. "You have not one, but *two* constraints," she said. "You committed to a two-week schedule, but your *budget* doesn't allow you to produce a 1,500-word piece in that timeframe. Your scope is too big for your budget. I suggest you limit the length of your posts to something you can accomplish within the time you set aside for blogging."

Brandon agreed. With these two constraints—schedule and budget—he needed to adjust the scope. He only had a few hours each week budgeted for blogging and couldn't neglect his other duties. "How long of a post can I write every two weeks?" he asked himself. After a month of experimentation, Brandon found that an optimal blog post was about 500 words. That was what he could do in two weeks—select a topic, research it, and write 500 words. If they were longer, he either exceeded his budget or couldn't post on time. He revised his approach of interviewing industry experts and instead relied on co-workers and previously published material. He trimmed the length but maintained much of the quality. He watched the analytics and concluded that his 500-word posts were just as effective as his longer ones. With Jill's help, Brandon had effectively balanced scope, schedule, and budget to launch a successful long-term blogging program.

Launch Lessons

- A project plan is the third and final launch engine that sets the course for your project.
- The scope, usually defined by the project's client or sponsor, is the *what*. It specifies objectives, tasks, and criteria.
- The approach, usually defined by the project team, is the *how*. It specifies methods, assumptions, and decisions making.

- The schedule is the *when*. It specifies deadlines and helps the team commit to on-time delivery.
- The budget describes the financial resources available to complete the project.
- These components of the project plan balance and check each other.

Action Items

Based on what I learned from this chapter, I will:

_____

_____

_____

_____

_____

_____

NOTES

[1] BrainyQuote, accessed January 17, 2017, https://www.brainyquote.com/quotes/quotes/p/pablopicas120939.html.

[2] See J. Richard Hackman, *Leading Teams: Setting the Stage for Great Performances* (Boston: Harvard Business Review Press, 2002).

[3] For more on these scheduling tools, see chapters 8 and 9 of *HBR Guide to Project Management* (Boston: Harvard Business Review Press, 2012).

[4] See, for example, Rick A. Morris and Brette McWhorter Sember, *Project Management That Works* (New York: American Management Association, 2008); Duncan Haughey, "Understanding the Project Management Triple Constraint," *Project Smart*, December 19, 2011; *Wikipedia*, s.v. "Project Management Triangle." Similar models add customer expectations, sustainability, and other quality constraints.

⁵ I-15 CORE project information comes from personal conversations with Todd Jensen, I-15 CORE director; Mark Shaw, "UDOT Completes I-15 CORE Project $260M Under Budget," *Engineering News-Record*, January 3, 2013; "Billion Dollar Baby," *Utah Construction & Design*, March 1, 2013; "Utah County I-15 Corridor Expansion (I-15 CORE) Design-Build," HDR Inc., http://www.hdrinc.com/portfolio/utah-county-i-15-corridor-expansion-i-15-core-design-build; HNTB, "I-15 Corridor Expansion," http://www.hntb.com/Projects/I-15-Corridor-Expansion.

Chapter 7

Launch Procedures

They would tell you that freedom lies in being cautious. Freedom lies in being bold.

ROBERT FROST[1]

You've defined a vision. You've formed a team. You've drafted a plan. When you feel you have enough to go on, it's time to plan a launch meeting.

You've already been working with your team and the client/sponsor informally to arrive at this point, so it's not a cold start. Still, the launch meeting, or kickoff meeting, is the official beginning. It has several purposes:

- Share the vision
- Begin teambuilding
- Define the plan
- Energize participants
- Establish norms of leadership and communication

Let's go over some launch procedures step by step. But first, a note on size. The procedures outlined here assume a reasonably large project and launch meeting. Your project might be smaller (or larger) and you'll want to adapt some of the recommendations. Still, the same launch engines apply: this is your primary opportunity to emphasize the vision, bring all team members together, and introduce the initial plan everyone will follow.

All Systems Go (Weeks to Launch)

Depending on the project, you may need 30 to 90 minutes for the launch meeting. You need enough time to explain the project, answer questions, build consensus, and bond. Don't rush through it, but also don't drag it out longer than necessary. Select a duration you think will allow you to bring everyone up to speed without discussing every item in detail. More time is recommended for out-of-town launch meetings where attendees will be traveling and need to make their trip worthwhile and interact face-to-face with team members.

Since late arrivals are inevitable, and because you want everyone to be there, I suggest you plan a few extra minutes at the beginning. Just make it part of the meeting—time for refreshments or visiting. You won't announce it as such, of course, since you want people to come on time. For example, you might set the meeting for 10:00, but realize that that's when people arrive and the mingling officially begins. You can start speaking at 10:15. I call this a "latecomer cushion." It serves the double purpose of allowing for delayed arrivals while offering some extra teambuilding time for those already present.

Choose a location that's most convenient for all participants. The venue should accommodate all attendees, allow for socializing, and offer furniture, lighting, and technology that meet your needs. Ideally, you or a teammate will be able to visit the venue before the event and work out the logistics. Determine how to best select or arrange the room:

- Conference: Single table; good for discussion and notetaking in small groups.
- Banquet: Small group tables; good for collaboration, computing, notetaking, and socializing.
- Auditorium: Rows of chairs facing a stage; good for long presentations, large groups, and limited space.
- Classroom: Rows of desks facing forward; good for long presentations, collaboration, computing, and notetaking.

These decisions will depend on the length of the meeting, the number of attendees, and what activities you are planning. Besides main seating, remember you may need to accommodate check-in, refreshments, displays, and equipment.

Finally, send invitations. I suggest at least one month's notice to avoid conflicts, and longer if travel will need to be arranged. You've already chosen your team, so the invitation shouldn't be the first they've heard of the project or their involvement in it. Along with the meeting details, include a personal message connected to the vision, like "As you know, we're going to develop a new system for environmental monitoring that will help improve safety and reliability. Please join us to launch this exciting project." To avoid Taylor's problem (Chapter 2), include everyone you think may be involved so they know who they're working with: the client/sponsor, external stakeholders, and your own team. Remember it's worth it to gather everyone at the beginning of a project, especially if some team members will be working remotely. Their physical presence at the beginning will establish personal connections that will continue through the project.

Countdown (Days to Launch)

In the days leading up to the launch meeting, I recommend the following.

Prepare an agenda. There are many variations (and many templates available online), but they look something like this:

- Welcome
- Project vision
- Project description
- Goals and deliverables
- Team member introductions and roles
- Project plan
- Communication protocol
- Q&A
- Conclusion
- Free time

You may also want to include food, a teambuilding activity, a brainstorming session, or remarks from the client/sponsor.

Prepare materials or handouts. Think project plans, posters, signups, shirts, nametags, pinback buttons, etc. Design these around the vision and use them as tools to foster unity and commitment.

Prepare your launch presentation. Advice on preparing and delivering outstanding presentations is plentiful; I recommend Nancy Duarte's *HBR Guide to Persuasive Presentations*.[2] Begin with the big idea—your vision, the *why*—and develop content to support it. Draft a few key points you want attendees to remember. Consider your presentation medium. A well-crafted slide deck is certainly an option, but a speech, story, or whiteboard presentation might be more effective depending on your message and audience. Choose the right tool for the job. Remember, you must explain your idea in just a few minutes and elicit both understanding and interest.

Launch Procedures

Practice your launch presentation. Out loud. And preferably in the launch venue. Work out all the transitions, controls, and logistics—you don't want to be fumbling with the lights or the microphone during the launch meeting. Watch your posture, timing, and tone. Imagine your audience—the ones who will help you fulfill the vision. You might practice on a colleague or even film yourself and watch for things to improve. There is no substitute for a real rehearsal, and the camera doesn't lie.

Remember that your presentation is probably at the mercy of fickle technology, so you should plan a contingency. I've seen well-prepared and otherwise captivating presentations undone by a lack of Wi-Fi, a burned-out projector bulb, or a podium computer that fails to recognize a USB device. Print a copy of your presentation that you could at least read in case of a total technological meltdown. Paper never fails. You might also prepare notecards, a whiteboard story, or other low-tech alternatives.

Consider some free time after the official meeting in order to continue the buzz and help participants become acquainted with each other. They could sign a banner or poster as a symbol of their commitment. You could offer refreshments and play music—a sort of reception. Perhaps a team photo is in order. Whatever you choose, it should be informal and organic, allowing participants to relax, socialize, and have fun before departing. Plan this activity to follow the official meeting.

Arrange for someone to photograph the event. The images can be used throughout the project to keep the launch engines burning and help tell your team's story.

On the night before the launch meeting, pack your launch equipment and materials. Also recommended: scissors, tape, paper, and markers. Set two alarm clocks and charge your phone.

Ignition (Launch Day)

On launch day, arrive well ahead of time to set up chairs, tables, agendas, nametags, signs, and refreshments. Test your equipment. Once you're set up, take a break to breathe and relax before the meeting starts. You might even strike a private Superman pose to boost confidence.[3] (Really.)

Start on time. If you've planned a latecomer cushion and really intend to start 15 minutes after the invited time, make sure that's clear on the agenda/schedule so people don't think you're behind before the meeting even begins. An on-time start shows that you're confident and organized, that you value the participants' time, and that you're excited to begin.

First, welcome everyone and introduce yourself. Point out exits, restroom locations, and other pertinent information about the venue. Briefly explain the agenda to orient participants. You may invite the sponsor/client to share some opening remarks.

Next, start your presentation. Share your vision. Tell the story of *why*: why the project exists, why it's important, and why you brought everyone here. Explain the need for the project and the impact it will have. If you already have one, share your vision statement. Then describe the project. What are you going to be doing? Outline the key goals and deliverables. Remember that this is not the time for details or discussion, but for understanding the big picture. You're communicating the vision and building consensus, as well as demonstrating leadership and enthusiasm.

Then turn to your team. Have everyone introduce themselves. I know how hackneyed this sounds—I heard you groan just now. As a college student I endured some 100 classes where, on the first day, we "went around the room and introduced ourselves." I always despised it because our relationship was temporary, it was an unproductive use of class time, and a quarter of the students dropped out after two days. While I did develop some great friendships in these classes (including with my wife), it was not because of the introductions alone but the interaction I had with certain classmates thereafter as we felt a commitment to help each other succeed. Until I needed a classmate's help (or vice versa), I was not interested in getting to know them. As soon as a mutual interdependence emerged in reaching a common goal, we became fast friends.

Now, in your launch meeting, is the time to introduce everyone. (If your gathering is too large to permit individual introductions, focus on key personnel or have neighbors introduce themselves to each other.) This will only be effective if 1) it occurs in the context of a common goal, 2) they realize their interdependence on each other, 3) they know no one will drop out, and 4) sufficient interaction follows in order to cement the relationships. They should ask themselves, "Where do I fit in all this?" Invite team members to *stand up* when they speak—visual identification is important, especially in large groups or large rooms. A microphone may or may not be necessary, but if you choose to use it, *use it*. (And require everyone to use it: all or nothing. Don't give in to people who claim to "have a loud voice and don't need the mic." If they have anything worth saying to the group, they should use the mic.) Have participants explain their role in the project in terms of fulfilling the vision, and relate it to the main goals and deliverables you outlined, as well as to each other:

> Hi, I'm Lee. I've worked here for six years and will be leading the coding effort for the environmental monitoring system we're developing. My role is to take the functional criteria that Nancy produces and translate them into Python algorithms to connect with the equipment Sam's group is building.

The purpose here is to reinforce the vision and roles "so that the weaving of seemingly unconnected actions can be clarified to understand how the parts form the whole."[4] You're helping team members connect the dots.

Once the introductions are over, move on to the project plan. Your team should be familiar with the basics by now; you may have already met with some of them informally or circulated a draft project plan before the meeting. As you present, emphasize that this is a draft, that much will change, and that you welcome feedback. It's a general strategy at this point, not a step-by-step recipe. Here, verify that the tasks, schedule, approach, and roles are reasonable and get everyone to agree on what's expected.

Now to communication. You'll need to define the frequency, mode, and involvement on various communication scales. Are weekly phone calls with the client sufficient? Do you need a monthly written progress report from each task leader? Will you share files externally through email, or through a secure FTP site? Should everyone be able to communicate with everyone, or do you prefer more defined channels? How should mistakes be brought to your attention? These are some of the questions you'll need to answer before your project takes off.

Once that's all settled, ask for feedback in a question-and-answer session. While it can be tempting to focus on your responses, focus instead on listening. One of Stephen Covey's seven habits is "Seek first to understand, then to be understood."[5] Show interest, pause before responding, repeat the question for the group if necessary, and speak calmly. If one person asks, chances are that others have the same question. Thank them for their interest and for allowing you to clarify for the whole group. Admit when you don't know the answer. Listen for hidden concerns lurking under an innocuous question, such as doubts about schedule or a personality conflict with a teammate. If the questions drift to tangents or minutiae, refocus the group's attention on the launch engines. You must balance the need to encourage and reassure participants and the need to address their legitimate concerns. If time runs out, offer to receive questions by phone or email after the meeting.

At the end, *briefly* reiterate the vision, team, and plan one last time with the same enthusiasm you began with. ("Brevity is the soul of wit," Shakespeare said.)[6] Announce the free time activities. Thank everyone for coming and close promptly and gracefully—no lengthy speeches. Mingle with participants during the free time.

Afterward, celebrate, debrief, and forge ahead.

Checklists

For convenience, the foregoing guidance on planning and running a launch meeting has been organized into a set of checklists found in the Appendix.

Launch Lessons

- Your project may not be as grand as a moon landing, but you'll need a powerful launch nonetheless.
- You don't need to have every detail planned at this point, just enough to take large steps in the right direction.
- For your launch presentation, there is no substitute for preparation and practice.
- Use the launch meeting to share the vision, strengthen the team, review the plan, energize participants, and demonstrate leadership.
- Use the checklists in the Appendix to guide you through this important process.

Action Items

Based on what I learned from this chapter, I will:

_____

_____

_____

_____

_____

_____

NOTES

[1] "A Conversation with Robert Frost," *NBC News* (New York: NBC Universal, November 23, 1952).

[2] Nancy Duarte, *HBR Guide to Persuasive Presentations* (Boston: Harvard Business Review Press, 2012).

[3] See Amy Cuddy's TED talk "Your Body Language Shapes Who You Are" (TEDGlobal, June 2012).

[4] Dale Christenson and Derek H. T. Walker, "Understanding the Role of 'Vision' in Project Success," *Project Management Journal* 35, no. 3 (September 2004), 40.

[5] Stephen R. Covey, *The 7 Habits of Highly Effective People: Powerful Lessons in Personal Change* (New York: Free Press, 1989).

[6] William Shakespeare, *Hamlet, Prince of Denmark*, ed. David Bevington and David Scott Kastan (New York: Bantam Dell, 2005), 2.2.90.

Chapter 8

Beyond the Launch

Faithless is he that says farewell
when the road darkens.

J. R. R. Tolkien[1]

W hile the launch is the official beginning, the three engines—vision, team, and plan—need to burn for some time afterward. It may be a long journey, and you'll need all the momentum you can muster. We've covered some of the points already, but we'll revisit them in the context of post-launch practices.

Vision Reinforcement

In Chapter 4 we learned the value of a project vision and its role in a successful launch. If regularly reinforced, it can continue to influence your project long afterward. Once a project is under way and specific tasks are assigned, it's all too easy for team members to look down and get lost in the details of their work. Let me illustrate with an experience shared by Adrián Ochoa, a church leader and family friend, from his childhood in Mexico:

> When I was eight, two cousins and I were sent to a nearby town to get groceries. ... The morning skies were bright and shiny as we departed in our small caravan of three horses.
>
> In the middle of the prairie, we had a brilliant idea that we should dismount and play marbles. So we did—for a long time. We were so absorbed in our game that we did not see the "signs of the times" above our heads as dark clouds covered the sky. By the time we realized what was happening, we didn't even have time to mount our horses. The heavy rain was hitting us so hard. ...
>
> Horseless, wet, and cold, we continued our journey, now trying to move as fast as we could. ... It was late at night when, tired and sore and soaked, we sought shelter in the first home we saw as we entered the town. The good young family there dried us off, fed us delicious bean burritos, and then put us to bed in a room of our own. Soon we discovered that the room had a flat dirt floor, so we had another brilliant idea. We drew a circle on the floor and continued our marbles game until we collapsed. ...
>
> If we had been wiser, we would have looked at the sky, spotted the clouds forming, and accelerated our pace to stay ahead of the storm. Now that I have a little more experience, I always remind myself, "Don't forget to look up."[2]

If you constantly focus on the task before you without looking up once in a while, you might drift off the path and be distracted. You may be very "efficient" working this way for a while, but then you realize that you're off course and caught in a storm, having spent days or weeks playing marbles while there was real work to be done. Besides costing time, such realizations can be very discouraging. The emotional consequences of looking down and forgetting the vision, whether intentionally or accidentally, are the more serious problem, like William in Chapter 1 or the Taurus workers in Chapter 4.

You and your team should "look up" at least once a week, both individually and as a group. Always ask yourselves, "Is this bringing us closer to fulfilling our vision? If so, how? If not, why?" Or, more memorably, "Are we playing marbles here?" You must convince yourselves that your current efforts and your vision are compatible. If there is any doubt, you need to resolve it sooner rather than later.

Invite team members to express their concerns to you if they sense any dissonance between their tasks and the vision. Imagine that a teammate comes to you and says, "The spreadsheet I've been working on is growing more complex by the day. I want to make sure this is what we really need to be doing. Can you help me understand how it fits with our vision?" On exploring such questions, you might discover that the spreadsheet's complexity doesn't support the vision, in which case it can be simplified and your teammate will be grateful that he asked the right question. Or you might determine that the complexity is indeed necessary to analyze data critical to your deliverable, in which case the work must continue and your teammate can proceed with full confidence that his effort is valuable. Either way, you are reinforcing the vision and its influence on everything you do, creating better performance and advancing you toward your goal in the long run.

The recommendations in Chapter 4 for internalizing the vision naturally apply after launch. The vision must become a regular part of your team's project experience. You can do this by including the vision statement in written project communications, preparing physical workplace reminders, referring to the vision in daily interactions, and demonstrating your own commitment to the vision in word and deed.

Don't forget to look up. When your team is deep in the details of their tasks, these practices will help them keep the big picture in mind for optimal project performance.

Team Development

Even after emphasizing the team before and during launch, it needs to develop into a powerful driving force. Your team requires attention well beyond launch and among many projects. But more than managing and delegating, you should be building the team's capacity to perform on this and future projects, like the Sowby Summit Team.

High-performing team members know their strengths. This sounds obvious, but I've been surprised at how some people are unaware of certain things they do really well. It could be that their strength is secondary to their core function or actual job title, like a secretary who happens to excel at data analysis or a doctor who happens to excel at marketing. Sometimes their strength *is* their primary function, but it's not noticed because it's diluted by being around so many others with the same job. I've witnessed several cases where an employee had strengths and added value in ways the management didn't seem to notice or appreciate because it wasn't the employee's main function. In *Apollo 13*, mission control director Gene Kranz says of the damaged spaceship that was meant to land on the moon but didn't: "I don't care what anything was *designed* to do, I care about what it *can* do." As project manager, you need to pay attention to what strengths your team members have and what they *can* do, regardless of what they were *hired* to do. If you only focus on their original purpose, you might miss an opportunity to have them boost the team in other ways. Help team members identify their own strengths and provide means for them to improve their strengths even more. This should be more than just passive observation, but rather active discovery and development of strengths.

As your project progresses, meet with team members individually to discuss strengths. Name their strengths and gauge their awareness of them: "Jen, I've noticed that you're really good at making charts. Have you ever noticed that? It's been a great strength to our team." Continue the conversation and get them to ponder that strength by asking them to tell you more. "How did you learn to make charts? Why is it important to you? How do you think charts help our project? Where else could your chart-making skills be used?" Show them how their strengths align with the project vision and their place on the team. Finally, ask if they could help other team members learn the same skills. "Jen, I think the whole team could benefit from some advanced chart-making tips. How would you like to host a one-hour workshop in a couple weeks?" This will boost their confidence, further hone their skills, and provide learning opportunities for the entire team.

Public recognition of strengths is important too. The team needs to hear you compliment individual members so they improve their team mentality and understand how complementary strengths make the team effective. Be careful, though: some people don't like too much attention and may feel embarrassed, or you might unequally praise certain people or skills, overlooking less obvious but equally important strengths. Be as equitable and as authentic as you can while doling out compliments.

Cross-training, where one team member learns to do the job of another, offers numerous benefits. This naturally follows the active discovery of strengths. Teaching someone a new skill makes the teacher view that skill from a new perspective and think critically about how the learner should approach it, reinforcing their own previous training and providing new insights that benefit the team. The collaboration enables new relationships to form that may not have otherwise. By learning each other's roles, your team will develop greater organizational awareness: an understanding of how each part fits together in the project's big picture. Cross-training makes your team more durable by allowing work to continue during absences when it would otherwise halt. Team members may have to leave temporarily or permanently for various reasons, both expected and unexpected, and cross-training ensures that the disruption is minimal. (In the arts, this is the purpose of an understudy—a performer who can replace someone in a critical role during an emergency. The show must go on!) Cross-training is especially important for long projects where staff turnover can be significant and a given role may change hands several times.[3] Cross-training allows you to harness internal talent on the current project and build capacity for future ones.

Global design firm IDEO, famous for its seemingly bottomless innovation capacity, leverages cross-training and cross-disciplinary capabilities in its project teams. CEO Tim Brown described IDEO employees as T-shaped people. "The vertical stroke of the 'T' is a depth of skill that allows them to contribute to the creative process. ... The horizontal stroke of the 'T' is the disposition for collaboration across disciplines. ... T-shaped people have both depth and breadth in their skills."[4]

Cross-training helps turn I-shaped workers—those with depth but no collaborative propensity—into T-shaped workers. They learn to listen to other points of view, build on each other's ideas, and produce synergistic solutions rather than settling for compromises. Consider dedicating a portion of your team's time to cross-training. Much of it will occur naturally as team members collaborate, but you may need to structure deeper training on certain skills. Great teams continue to learn. They hone skills in their individual areas of expertise and also learn basic management, communication, and interdisciplinary skills that benefit everyone. You should provide the means for them to thrive.

Even if you start with a superb team, conditions can vary and you may need to reconsider who participates. Sometimes team membership must change for the benefit of the project. A lack of skills or performance must be addressed by bringing in someone new. I've joined several engineering projects midway because a need arose for skills that existing team members didn't have. I've also experienced the opposite, where someone else joined the team to bail me out. On the other hand, freeriders who want the benefits of team membership but don't contribute must be released. My wife has had to "fire" underperforming eight-year-old piano students who weren't committed (or whose parents weren't committed) to the piano studio team; I nearly dismissed a senior colleague from a committee I chaired because he wanted to be involved but wasn't adding any value. Don't shake up the team too often, though: people develop norms for working together, and frequent changes can hamper productivity.

Continue to promote team development in terms of performance, skills, and trust. Meet regularly so team members see each other contributing. Solicit their feedback on how things are going and brainstorm about where to go next. Hold occasional social events, both on-site and off-site, to promote familiarity on more than just a project level. These actions will help keep the team engine burning throughout the project.

Checking Plan Alignment

Review the project plan regularly to check progress and alignment on scope, approach, schedule, and budget.

"Scope creep" or "project creep" occurs when the project swells beyond its original boundaries. It often happens so subtly you might not notice. This happens when Christie launches parties, Christmas presents, and home decorating projects. At first it sounds innocuous enough: "Let's have a few neighbors over for dessert next Saturday." We think we'll prepare one type of dessert and confine the casual gathering to our rear patio. In reality, it becomes a full-blown reception featuring an incredible self-catered spread in a vigorously cleaned and impeccably decorated house where Christie and I perform a piano duet to entertain a hundred guests.

While fun and inconsequential in this setting, scope creep threatens many projects, especially those with finite budgets or schedules. Even seemingly small, innocent additions can ultimately topple a project. Speaking from firsthand experience, this slippery slope is also responsible for delaying many graduate theses and dissertations. Regularly review the scope to make sure that you're not adding anything extra—or leaving anything out. Be firm with your client/sponsor when they ask for extras that could take away from the defined work. Refer them to the scope you both agreed upon and committed to before the project started.

While it's important to control the scope (and thereby the budget and schedule), you must be able to recognize major opportunities that can add value. Don't focus so much on your predefined scope that you're blind and unresponsive to other chances to improve the project's quality or to secure further work. You should establish a procedure for evaluating scope changes and modifying the scope with a formal request or amendment. If certain items simply won't fit, don't just wave them away. If they came up, they must be valuable to someone. Keep a list of potential follow-up projects to consider later.

For checking approach alignment, ask yourself two questions: "Are we doing it the way we said we would?" and "Is this approach working?" Comparing your current methods with those you planned can be revealing. You may find that you've drifted into old bad habits. You may find that your awesome-on-paper approach isn't working as expected. You may find that you've actually come up with a totally new approach that is better than what you had proposed. Whatever the outcome, you can either be confident that you're doing the right thing or will be able to recognize the need to adjust. Revisit your vision and ask yourself if there is now a better way to get there than there was before.

If schedule is the critical constraint for your project, you need to check in regularly—weekly or daily, perhaps—to ensure that tasks are progressing adequately. You can't expect that things will run smoothly while you're engaged elsewhere. The more frequently you check in, the faster you can identify and resolve delay-causing problems. When a task falls behind, find out why. Is scope creep occurring or is the work more detailed than it needs to be? Are you missing certain data? Are team members not communicating well? Does your team lack the space, tools, and materials it needs to work efficiently? There are innumerable explanations, each which require a custom resolution. But if you don't investigate, you probably won't be able to reclaim the schedule.

Current tasks are your immediate focus, but don't be shortsighted. Also look ahead to future tasks to determine what steps are necessary before they can begin and to ensure that the right people, funds, and other resources will be in place so the task can begin as soon as possible.

Coming in under budget is the dream of most project managers, and it's directly related to scope, approach, and schedule. But it doesn't happen automatically, even after a powerful launch. Like the other plan components, it should be monitored regularly in order to detect any problems right away. During the project, look for unexpected opportunities to beat the budget: automation, outsourcing, bulk purchasing, partnering, and piggybacking are a few possibilities. I'll speak to the first: automation. In one of my early consulting projects, I came to a tedious and time-intensive data-entry task. The program I was using was not designed to easily accept the amount of data I was feeding it from my spreadsheet, so I had to manually enter the information in a series of small dialog boxes that required a dozen clicks each and were easily mixed up. After a few hours, I realized that it was ridiculous (and irresponsible) to charge the client expensive engineering fees for this menial service. Besides, I had had enough. I approached a programmer co-worker and asked if he saw a way forward. He wasn't familiar with my program but together we found that it used a plain-text input file to populate those annoying dialog boxes. With a few hours, he had studied the file format, written some code, and published a web-based tool that converted my entire spreadsheet into an input file the program could read. I estimated that this automation, though unexpected, saved about three weeks of the schedule, six percent of the budget, and an incalculable amount of my sanity.

Course Corrections

Turbulence and new information will necessitate course corrections. Both are inevitable, but you can manage them effectively and revise your project plan accordingly.

Turbulence is a natural consequence of flying. No matter how experienced the pilot is, she cannot turn off the turbulence or change the wind or stop the rain. Longfellow wrote:

> Be still, sad heart! and cease repining;
> Behind the clouds is the sun still shining;
> Thy fate is the common fate of all,
> Into each life some rain must fall. [5]

Turbulence during or after launch can spook even the best teams. You have three options: blast ahead, abort, or adjust course. Blasting ahead only makes rough air rougher, and aborting doesn't move you toward your goal. You must adjust course.

Besides dealing with turbulence, your project plan is imperfect from the beginning. You don't know everything and can't predict exact conditions and outcomes. New insights learned along the way will require you to adapt. Some of these insights will come from mistakes and failures, and others will come from fluctuating market conditions or organizational goals. Whatever the cause, you may need to revise your plan, repeat some work, backtrack, or even switch team members. Your course will have many turns, obstacles, and dead ends. You'll still get there, just by a different path than you imagined. Remember Goethe's perspective:

> Each path to a noble end
> Is also noble 'round each bend.[6]

One of the best tools for keeping your project on track is debriefing. Also called an after-action review or a lessons-learned meeting, debriefing is a structured learning process that helps you evaluate and correct course during the project. It's a meeting, it's an evaluation, it's a learning exercise, and it's a course corrector. You assemble your team for a frank conversation about what worked, what didn't, what you'll do to fix it. I recommend debriefing after completing project milestones like the launch meeting, major tasks, deliverables, and closeout. Or you may choose to debrief at regular intervals, perhaps weekly or monthly, depending on your project. If it's a long project, certain memories may fade over time and some team members may come and go before the end, so you need to capture their insight before it's too late.

For a debriefing to be effective, you must create an environment where learning matters more than blame, solutions matter more than errors, and the future matters more than the past. Uncomfortable conversations may arise, but the value of correcting mistakes and avoiding the same ones in the future outweighs any discomfort. Keep the discussion open and honest. You're all on the same team here, working toward the same objective. Teams who debrief regularly tend to have stronger relationships, communicate more effectively, and align more on purpose.[7]

What should you ask in a debriefing? You'll find many templates online, some of which are dizzyingly complex. Each project requires its own level of specificity depending on what needs to be evaluated. Leadership and strategy consultant Doug Sundheim recommended these four broad questions:[8]

1. What were we trying to accomplish?
2. Where did we hit (or miss) our objectives?
3. What caused our results?
4. What should we start, stop, or continue doing?

In these discussions, try to point out three things you did will and one thing you could improve. You will learn fastest by focusing on what you did *right*. Take careful notes to capture the lessons learned for later use. The outcome of these debriefings will inform course corrections: revisions to your project plan (and perhaps even your team and vision) that move you closer to your destination. The Wright Brothers debriefed after every flight, modifying their designs and practicing their maneuvers until everything was in order. The process will become easier and more valuable the more often you debrief.

The debriefing process is only valuable if you actually learn from it. When the project ends, rather than bury the notes in the project file, save them in a central repository—perhaps with your organization's project management office (PMO), if you have one—where anyone can find and study them. Over time you'll build a strong "debriefing data-base" or "lessons-learned library" that can inform future projects. To improve the odds of finding the right course, commit to reviewing notes from relevant past projects before launching a new one.

We Turn the Page

By writing *Learn to Launch* I launched a project about launching pro-jects. That's like solving a problem about problem solving or making a website about how to make websites: a curiously circular but insightful perspective that makes you think twice about what you're doing and whether you really practice what you preach. Was I fueling my book project with the same engines I was writing about in that very book?

Yes I was. At first I had only a vision: "Write a book that helps people successfully launch their own projects" or something like that, but it was enough to start with. I refined this vision to include a word count (about 30,000), a discussion of the three engines, and a mix of anecdotes, research, and poetry. I even imagined a six-inch by nine-inch paperback with an orange cover as a finished product.

But even with a cogent vision, I had no team and no plan to help it take off. Then I realized I did have a teammate: my wife, Christie, who has successfully launched many of her own projects and understood by experience the principles I would write about. Teammates on most things by default, Christie and I enjoy working together and have formed over time a valuable partnership that has led us through many projects. Yes, I wanted her on my team for this one.

We then formed a plan: settle on the topic, outline the content, conduct the research, and write the book between semesters in my Ph.D. program at the University of Utah. It certainly didn't proceed perfectly. Sometimes my enthusiasm made me get ahead of myself. Sometimes I scrapped and rewrote entire chapters. Sometimes I felt overwhelmed and frustrated. But the vision and team pulled me through, and the plan was good enough.

With the book nearing completion now, I feel my satisfaction growing. I've learned a lot (as I always do when writing)[9] and worked on something meaningful to me. Soon I'll be able to say that I wrote a book—a definite stretch goal and a fulfillment of my vision. Now I'll turn my attention to my next project: raising a daughter.

The delivery and closeout of a project can be an emotionally charged experience. You've invested incredible amounts of time, energy, and passion to pursue a vision that mattered to you. You've developed a proficient team and meaningful relationships. You've executed a great plan, perhaps not perfectly, but it worked. You overcame the challenges and learned much. Your project succeeded.

And it's all over. Now what?

First, you celebrate. Gather your team for a lunchtime fiesta, hold a ribbon-cutting ceremony, or give out some branded novelties—whatever it is you do to reward a job well done. Congratulate each person for his or her contributions to meeting the objectives. The celebration needs to be separate from performance reviews or debriefings: this part is fun, not business. Even if the project wasn't great, you all worked hard and deserve to celebrate what you did right. Let your team enjoy their accomplishments.

Second, there's always another project—maybe not in your profession, and maybe not the same size, but it's out there waiting for you. You might pursue one of those scope creep items that didn't quite fit the first time. Maybe you'll spin off a side project. Perhaps you'll launch a second phase to develop more features or add other value to the original project. Going on a family vacation? Organizing a charity event? Raising a child? How about another BHAG? (Remember that your peak is the best time to pursue another stretch goal.) Whatever it is, the same principles apply.

In 1950, French mountaineers Maurice Herzog and Louis Lachenal were the first to reach the summit of an 8,000-meter (26,500-foot) peak—a vertical boundary known as the death zone. Their ascent of the Himalayan massif Annapurna, the world's tenth-highest peak, was particularly remarkable given that the mountain was explored, surveyed, and climbed—without supplemental oxygen—in a single season. Though the expedition's nine members had suffered greatly due to poor information and other setbacks, the team had coalesced around the vision and planned a way forward. Their summiting was the achievement of a lifetime, a feat few thought was possible.

Herzog documented the experience in his book *Annapurna*. It recounts one of the greatest adventures of all time and has sold more copies than any other mountaineering title. Reflecting on the experience, Herzog wrote:

> For every one of us, Annapurna was an ideal that had been realized. ...
> Annapurna, to which we had gone emptyhanded, was a treasure on which we should live the rest of our days. With this realization we turn the page: a new life begins.
> There are other Annapurnas in the lives of men.[10]

As with "other Annapurnas," one project builds on another. Neil Armstrong, the first man to walk on the moon, was deeply influenced by the Wright brothers, those monumental pioneers of flight from his home state. "As a boy, because I was born and raised in Ohio, about 60 miles north of Dayton, the legends of the Wrights have been in my memories as long as I can remember," he said. Armstrong, who had flown farther from Earth than anyone but a handful of other Apollo astronauts, marveled at how far aviation had come in just a few decades. "I guess that's the story of flight in the 20th century: from the beginning, the very first flights at Kitty Hawk to the various, very furthest and fastest flights that man has ever made."[11] On his trip to the moon, Armstrong carried a swatch of fabric from the wing of the Wright Brothers' original plane.[12]

Apollo 11's lunar excursion module, Eagle, *returns from the lunar surface, with an "earthrise" in the background, July 21, 1969. This photo and others represent the fulfillment of a vision.*

In 1999, in a press conference celebrating the 30th anniversary of the moon landing, Armstrong was asked what he saw as the lasting legacy of the Apollo program. His unrehearsed reply was profound. "The important achievement of Apollo was a demonstration that humanity is not forever chained to this planet," he said. "Our visions go rather further than that, and our opportunities are unlimited."[13]

Your recently completed project may leave you with similar sentiments: deep appreciation for the experience and the will to press on.

Where will you go next?

Launch Lessons

- Continually reinforce the vision in meetings, communications, and personal interactions.
- Strengthen your team in both professional and personal ways throughout the project.
- Regularly check alignment with your scope, schedule, approach, and budget.
- Debrief after project milestones, correct course if necessary, and recognize individual contributions.
- When one project is done, be grateful, enjoy the moment, and use the momentum to drive another.

Action Items

Based on what I learned from this chapter, I will:

_____

_____

_____

_____

_____

NOTES

[1] J. R. R. Tolkien, *The Lord of the Rings* (London: HarperCollins, 1994), 274.

[2] Adrián Ochoa, "Look Up," *Ensign*, November 2013, 102–103.

[3] I discuss this further in another article. See Robert B. Sowby, "Handling Your First Multi-Year Project," *Project Times*, February 13, 2015.

[4] Morten T. Hansen, "IDEO CEO Tim Brown: T-Shaped Stars: The Backbone of IDEO's Collaborative Culture," *Chief Executive*, January 21, 2010. Also see Chris Cancialosi, "Cross-Training: Your Best Defense against Indispensable Employees," *Forbes*, September 15, 2014.

[5] Henry Wadsworth Longfellow, "The Rainy Day," in *Henry Wadsworth Longfellow*, selected by Anthony Thwaite (Phoenix Poetry, 2003), 37.

[6] Robert B. Sowby, ed., trans., *Johann Wolfgang von Goethe: Proverbs* (2014), 14.

[7] Doug Sundheim, "Debriefing: A Simple Tool to Help Your Team Tackle Tough Problems," *Harvard Business Review*, July 2, 2015.

[8] Sundheim, "Debriefing."

[9] I have discovered over the years that writing is my best learning tool. It forces me to develop, organize, and present my thoughts in a way that makes sense to me and my readers.

[10] Maurice Herzog, *Annapurna: The First Conquest of an 8,000-Meter Peak*, trans. Nea Morin and Janet Adam Smith (Guilford, CT: Lyons Press, 2010), 223.

[11] Miles O'Brien, "The Wright Stuff," *CNN*, December 17, 2002. The online version appears to have been posted about one year later, December 16, 2003.

[12] David McCullough, *The Wright Brothers* (New York: Simon & Shuster, 2015), 262.

[13] "Apollo 11 30th Anniversary Press Conference," July 16, 1999, NASA History Program Office, https://history.nasa.gov/ap11ann/pressconf.htm.

Appendix

Launch Checklists

The following checklists supplement the material presented in Chapter 7, Launch Procedures. Refer to the chapter for explanation and detail.

Vision Statement

Write your vision statement here and plan all launch activities around it:

_____

_____

_____

_____

_____

All Systems Go (Weeks to Launch)

☐ Find a helper to assist in the meeting arrangements.

☐ Select a location and venue that will accommodate your group's size, technology, furniture, and travel needs.

☐ If possible, visit the venue.

☐ Schedule the launch meeting with 1–2 months' notice to all who will need to attend.

☐ Send invitations to all participants.

Countdown (Days to Launch)

☐ Prepare an agenda.

☐ Prepare relevant vision-centered materials and handouts:

    ☐ Project plans

    ☐ Posters/banners

    ☐ Nametags

    ☐ Souvenirs

☐ Arrange for client/sponsor remarks.

☐ Prepare vision-centered launch presentation.

☐ Practice presentation. (Recording and evaluation recommended.)

☐ Prepare low-tech presentation backup, e.g., hard copy, notecards, or whiteboard (bring your own markers).

☐ Plan post-launch activity, e.g., reception, photo, or teambuilding.

☐ Arrange for someone to take photos of the event.

☐ Send a meeting reminder.

☐ On the night before the launch meeting:

    ☐ Pack your launch equipment and materials. Also recommended: scissors, tape, paper, and markers.

    ☐ Set two alarm clocks! And get a good night's sleep.

    ☐ Charge your phone.

Ignition (Launch Day)

☐ Eat a healthy breakfast.

☐ Arrive early.

☐ Set up tables, chairs, signs, handouts, and/or refreshments.

☐ Test your equipment and presentation.

☐ Escape and relax for a few minutes before the meeting starts.

☐ Start on time!

☐ Launch!

    ☐ Welcome everyone.

    ☐ Introduce yourself.

    ☐ Announce logistics: parking, restrooms, exits, etc.

    ☐ Outline the agenda.

    ☐ Invite client/sponsor to share remarks.

    ☐ Give your best, well-rehearsed, energetic, vision-centered launch presentation.

    ☐ Introduce the team. Have each stand and explain his or her role.

    ☐ Share the project plan.

    ☐ Define communication protocol.

    ☐ Conduct Q&A session. Listen! Respond as best you can, but stick to the big picture.

    ☐ Close gracefully by mentioning the vision one last time and thanking participants for coming. Announce any post-launch activity.

☐ Take photos.

☐ Celebrate!

☐ Debrief.

Acknowledgments

I t is a pleasure for me to acknowledge others' roles in helping me prepare *Learn to Launch*. My wife, Christie, was a sounding board for my ideas and provided several insights and anecdotes from her own experience in piano performance, music education, and professional organizations. She was an invaluable teammate who encouraged me throughout the process since it was clearly something I cared about. My father, Stephen Ellis Sowby, a civil engineer like me, nurtured my technical interests. My mother, Laurie Williams Sowby, a lifetime journalist, nurtured my artistic interests and helped edit this manuscript.

I thank many local leaders of The Church of Jesus Christ of Latter-day Saints, including Jeffrey R. Robbins, Robert T. Smith, David L. Kezerian, and Lowell V. Smith, who allowed me to personally observe their leadership in public and private meetings and practice my launch skills in church and social settings. Many other church associates in the Forest Bend LDS Ward inspired me in other ways.

My engineering colleagues at Hansen, Allen & Luce were excellent leadership specimens and allowed me to contribute to many engineering projects while learning about project management and developing my own technical skills. The firm has been a laboratory for me to learn and test project management ideas.

My advisor at the University of Utah, Dr. Steven J. Burian, helped me form a vision—over several iterations—for my doctoral work in civil engineering and steered me back to that vision when I veered off to explore other interesting but distracting ideas. He was a noble teammate and guided me through a difficult research plan.

It is from and with these people, and countless others unnamed, that I learned by experience many of the concepts documented in this book.

About the Author

A water resources engineer, musician, author, and world traveler, Robert B. Sowby has observed or managed the launches of over 100 projects from software development to infrastructure design. He has also applied the principles of *Learn to Launch* to projects at home, school, and church. Rob studied at Brigham Young University, Massachusetts Institute of Technology, Harvard University, and the University of Utah. He lives in Salt Lake City with his wife, Dr. Christie Sowby, a professional pianist.

www.ingramcontent.com/pod-product-compliance
Lightning Source LLC
Chambersburg PA
CBHW030007190526
45157CB00014B/921